Great
Quilting
Techniques

from **Threads**

Great Quilting Techniques

from *Threads*

The Taunton Press

Taunton
BOOKS & VIDEOS
for fellow enthusiasts

First printing: January 1994
Printed in the United States of America

A THREADS Book

THREADS® is a trademark of The Taunton Press, Inc.,
registered in the U.S. Patent and Trademark Office.

The Taunton Press
63 South Main Street
Box 5506
Newtown, CT 06470-5506

Library of Congress Cataloging-in-Publication Data

Great quilting techniques from Threads.
        p.   cm.
    "A Threads book" — CIP t.p. verso.
    Includes index.
    ISBN 1-56158-070-8
    1. Quilting.
TT834.G734   1993   93-27564
    746.46 — dc20   CIP

Contents

Introduction

*t*here are no limits to fabric application in the quilting world. And no magazine explores the potential of fabric more than *Threads* magazine. From stuffing and painting to stitching, stippling and staining, this selection of quilting articles will add excitement to your fabric toolbox.

In the following pages, artists and designers share their techniques for appliquéing perfect points, adding realism and depth to monochromatic cloth, turning ties into wearable art, and patchworking without patterns. Whether you're making a quilted coat, or piecing, appliquéing or embellishing a quilted surface, this information from *Threads* offers the tools you need for the best results.

Amy T. Yanagi, editor

A Passion for Piecing

Hand-stitched curves, appliqué, and kimono silks make knockout quilts

by Kumiko Sudo

When I was a nine-year-old girl in Japan, my mother and I made a collage diary, which consisted of all types of pictures and unusual designs. I loved making new designs and patterns as a child, and it is something I will continue to do all my life in my quilting.

Even though I now live and work in America, it is impossible for me to forget my Japanese background, and the feelings I have about Japan are often reflected in my work, as you can see in the quilts shown in the photos on the facing page and on p. 11.

Throughout Japan's long history, its society has been concerned with dress, and in old Japan costume automatically signified one's social position. Certain colors and design patterns had symbolic meaning, and there were rules about what clothing, colors, and fabrics could be worn together.

The influence of this history survives in modern society and forms part of my cultural heritage. It makes my approach different from traditional quilting and gives my quilts their character.

From idea to color and cloth

Whenever a new design begins in my mind, I immediately make a small sketch, and after a while I make a larger drawing. At this stage I still keep modifying the design, and when I am finally satisfied with it, I make a full-size line drawing of it on a large sheet of paper.

I hang this full-size drawing on the wall in my studio. For a number of days I see it as I come and go and make final changes I feel are appropriate.

Choosing the colors is one of the most important and exciting steps—the selection of colors depends a great deal upon my feelings at the moment. The time of year or the weather of a particular day has an influence on the colors I choose.

For more than fifteen years while I lived in Japan, I collected kimono and obi from many different places. When I first came to this country, I used silk from these old Japanese garments to make many of my quilts. I still use silks, but it is hard for me to cut up the clothing so I use more of the scraps that are left from making new kimono. I have a collection of these scraps and samples of kimono silk that I got from kimono makers in Japan. I now also use other fabrics like cottons in my pieces.

I buy fabrics two or so yards at a time, whenever I see a color, pattern, or print I think I'd like to work with. There is a large table in my studio on which I store these quilt fabrics so they'll always be in plain sight. I fold them in a uniform size and stand them up in rows so I can see them all at once. By grouping them by color family, I can see at a glance which shade is exactly right for my purpose.

After I have decided the major colors for the work I am involved with, I pick out those colors from my fabric collection and spread them on the floor. From this array of fabric I choose the colors and patterns that will best fit the design and spirit of the work.

Putting it all together

I usually appliqué my quilts to a white base fabric, so the first step is to transfer the pattern from the full-size drawing to the base. I like to use old sheets for the base fabric, and I ask my family and friends to save their sheets for me. Sometimes I can find them in second-hand stores.

Once I finish the drawing on the base fabric, the real work begins. My designs use few repeated shapes, so I have to make a separate template for nearly every design element. Even my small quilts can have hundreds of pieces, and each piece may have its own template.

First I trace one pattern area from the drawing and cut out the shape. Then I use the tracing paper as a template and copy the finished size of the pattern onto white cardboard. After adding a seam allowance, I cut the cardboard on the outer line. I cut the center from the cardboard shape with a rotary cutter and cutting mat, making a window.

With the window, I can place the pattern piece on the fabric to see exactly how it will look in the finished quilt, as I am doing in the center photo on p. 10. Sometimes, by rotating the window, I

Curved piecing is a hallmark of author Kumiko Sudo's quilting. This detail of "Temari" (34½ in. by 47 in., 1988) shows her intricate curves and the embroidery stitching she prefers to the usual quilting stitch. Each piece of the quilt is hand stitched to a kimono silk backing fabric with silk thread. (Photo courtesy of the author)

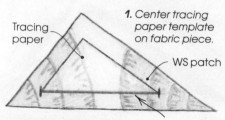

Tracing paper

1. Center tracing paper template on fabric piece.

WS patch

2. Mark one seamline with chalk, clearly marking ends.

3. Mark matching stitching line on piece to be joined.

4. Pin together, stabbing pins through marked lines.

WS   RS   RS

5. Sew, securing ends of stitching as shown.

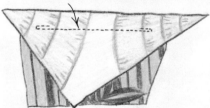

6. Replace tracing paper; mark second seam. Mark next piece to be joined; pin and stitch as before.

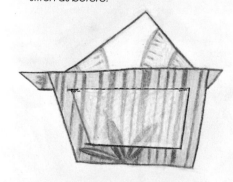

Repeat this marking and sewing sequence to complete piecing the points, then stitch to base fabric.

In the first step in making a window template, the author traces a shape from her full-size drawing (above).

After adding seam allowances and cutting out the template, she chooses the fabric design to cut for the quilt (shown at left).

Placing the fabric piece on a sheet of sandpaper to keep it from shifting, Sudo marks the first line for hand stitching (below).

Illustrations by Mary Smith

In her abstract "Picture Scrolls," Sudo shows us two ladies of the court passing their leisure time in playing cards. The beautiful printed fabrics of their costumes indicate their standing in the aristocracy, and the black areas are their flowing hair tucked away inside the layers of kimono in the fashion of the time. (48½ in. by 29½ in.; 1989; photo courtesy of the author)

find combinations of colors and shapes I would not see otherwise.

After I cut the pieces on the outside line, I hand stitch them one at a time to the base fabric. I try to start with the background pieces and work toward the foreground, and since the edges of the back pieces will be covered by those in front, I leave them unfinished. To apply the foreground pieces, I turn the raw edges under and slip-stitch them in place invisibly. All of my sewing is done by hand, using only Japanese silk thread. I use it for quilting, too. The silk thread that I use is Daruma brand, but all the Japanese silk thread brands are similar; both of the suppliers listed in Sources at right carry other good brands.

I like curved lines and work them into my designs much more often than straight geometric pieces. When I do use straight lines and have several corners coming together at one point, I change my technique a little. Instead of appliquéing the pieces down individually, I patch them together so the corners will be neat and sharp. The method I use is shown in the drawing and photo on the facing page. Then I sew the group of pieces to the base fabric as a unit.

After the whole piece is sewn to the backing, I hang the completed picture on the wall for a few days or longer. This way I can check to make sure the design is just the way I want it. Changes are easier to make at this stage than in the finished quilt, so if a patch is not right I can take it off and replace it.

Batting, quilting, and lining

Most of my works are made to be wall hangings. I treat them differently than I would if they were to be used on beds. For many of them, I iron heavy fusible interfacing directly onto the back of the base fabric, and this is all the filling I use. For others, I insert a thin batting, like garment batting, between the base fabric and the lining.

Quilting for me is part of design and decoration, rather than something to be seen all over the picture, so I use stitching for accents. In quilts about Japanese people, I often take my designs from the family crests of the persons involved. I do use quilting and embroidery stitches to add details like facial features or flower centers to my pictures.

After all the piecing and decorative stitching is done, I line the quilt. I use only kimono lining silk and choose colors that will harmonize with the patchwork of the front of the quilt. I put the lining on by basting it in place through all the layers with cotton thread, then turning in the raw edges and slip-stitching them together with silk thread. After slip-stitching, I remove the basting. □

Kumiko Sudo discovered quilting on a visit to the United States and returned to Japan to start her own quilting and crafts school. Now residing in the U.S., she teaches in such places as the Quilt Festival in Houston, TX. Her book Expressive Quilts, *which shows more of her exquisite patchwork, is available from Pegasus Publishing, 87326 Green Hill Rd., Eugene, OR 97402.*

Sources for Japanese silk thread

Things Japanese
9805 N.E. 116th St.; Suite 7160
Kirkland, WA 98034
(206) 821-2287

Kasuri Dyeworks
1959 Shattuck Ave.
Berkeley, CA
(415) 841-4509

In the Nature of a Curve

How to fit spirals, arcs, and circles into a rectangle

by Martha Waterman

*P*erhaps it is because I love the marking and stitching of quilts as much as top-making that Welsh quilting designs first attracted me. I prefer to think that it's my Welsh ancestry coming to the fore—an ancient preference for curves over straight lines that has been preserved in my genes. But any quilt-maker can find new quilting interest in the nature-inspired curves and spirals of traditional Welsh quilting designs.

The hallmark of a traditional Welsh quilt is its flamboyant wealth of curvaceous quilting patterns. Piecing is minimal and the pieces tend to be large and often solid colored, so traditional Welsh quilts are frequently dismissed as everyday. But I think that Welsh quilters felt as I do, that quilting designs can be a large portion of a quilt's overall design. Complicated piecing detracts from the visual impact of quilting designs, and seams are difficult to quilt through. Whole-cloth quilts or those with a minimum of piecing give the quilting designs pride of place. There is also a deeper pride in Welsh reluctance to use patchwork, which seems to stem from a time when patchwork meant poverty and "making do." Whole-cloth quilts, strippies (made of wide, solid strips), and medallions—all typical Welsh patterns—were a way to show, without bragging, that one had the wherewithall to purchase beautiful fabric, often fine wool flannel, just for a quilt.

Circles, spirals, and curves

Sinuous curves, freehand spirals, circles, and half-circle motifs abound in Welsh quilting designs. They are, of course, part of the Celtic culture. You can see them deeply incised on the large standing stones that remain from primitive times all over Wales, Cornwall, Brittany, Ireland, and the west of Scotland (see the photo on p. 16). In fact, extraordinary circular motifs have been left by practically every culture in the world.

What is it about circles, spirals, and curves that appeals so deeply to almost all of us, no matter what our roots? Perhaps it's the dynamic potential of the shape. It suggests wholeness and completeness, but also great potential.

When Martha Waterman discovered the circles and curves of Welsh quilting, she also began to explore Welsh folklore and history. Both unite in the center of the pieced stars of "Owain Glyndŵer," named for the "last native prince of Wales," who was a keen astronomer and astrologer. (Photos, pp. 12-14, by Susan Kahn)

In "Cymru Am Byth" you can see typical Welsh quilting eccentricity, complete with snail. In one of the red strips, Waterman disrupted the traditional leaf design by reversing alternate leaves and setting a large spiral above each pair to produce a roselike image.

Although we don't know the exact purpose of the giant standing-stone circles that remain throughout the Celtic lands, they were obviously places of great importance, aligned to the movement of the sun and moon. Symbolically, the circle was important as the shape of the sun and moon, the moving forces of the universe. It was a symbol of wholeness and continuity—day following night, night following day unceasingly. The circle also carried with it the concept of equality, part of the Legend of King Arthur (a famous Welshman) and his Knights of the Round Table. So it's not surprising that the circle forms the basis of many Welsh quilting designs.

The freehand spiral is probably the most notable Welsh quilting design shape. Snails, seashells, whirlwinds—the spiral was observed in nature (perhaps also in archetypal dreams) and carved upon stone everywhere throughout the Celtic lands. It is so frequently seen that many scholars have speculated upon its symbolism. Most feel it represents the turn of time, the cyclical ebb and flow of the seasons and of birth, growth, death, and rebirth. Sometimes spiral shapes are called "snails" or "snail creep."

Leaf and fern shapes appear often in Welsh quilting in a somewhat stylized form. These natural decorations have also been found on Welsh stone carvings and ornaments from pagan times.

I made the vines on the white bands of "True Thomas," on p. 14, by folding paper the length and width of each strip to be filled and cutting it in a shallow S-shaped curve. Unfolded, this paper formed the repeating curve of the vine. And I cut the leaves, ferns, and flowers by hand from paper the size of the shapes to be filled. Then I traced sturdier plastic templates from them. Many leaf designs are drawn from overlapping half-circles. You'll find the process on p. 15. Their veining, however, is one of the few straight-line designs found in Welsh quilting. It mirrors the "Tree of Life" knitting patterns that are so often seen in the traditional fishermen's sweaters of Wales, Scotland, Ireland, and England.

Quilt design

As late as Victorian times, itinerant quilt markers and hand quilters, many of whom were men, traveled Wales selling or trading their skills and patterns. This may explain the similarity one finds among the quilting patterns on old quilts. But an even simpler explanation could be that many of the patterns are easily drawn using simple household objects like cups, saucers, or plates as the main template and filling in the rest by eye. Nearly every home in Wales did and does display a "Welsh Dresser" (in America, a hutch) filled with beautiful delft and china—a ready source for curves. Having seen the designs on family quilts or neighbors' beds, it would not be difficult for a woman to mark her own versions with the tools at hand.

There is great individuality in the marking of old Welsh quilts. Michele Walker (see "Further reading," below right) believes that "strippies" were marked a strip at a time in the frame. Other quilts show such an ingenious overall pattern that one assumes they were marked as a whole. The process that I used to mark "True Thomas," shown below, section by section and shape by shape is also a traditional Welsh method; the designs reflect a Scots, rather than Welsh, legend. Whole-cloth quilt tops were often divided into center squares, vertical bands, and borders, as the quilting on them plainly shows. Allover designs like "Hanging Diamond" or "Broken Plaid" did not appeal. Each pattern is a new marking and quilting challenge and an opportunity for self-expression and virtuosity.

The very popular *medallion quilt* was often made with a solid-colored center and several pieced borders, as opposed to the more common chintz or pictorial-fabric centers found elsewhere. The solid colors offered a large showcase for the elaborate quilting that was so prized. You can find an example of a center square design at top left on p. 16. I used this technique for the central medallion of my little ribbon star quilt, "Owain Glyndŵr," shown on p. 12.

Wide, vertical whole-cloth strips were used to make many Welsh quilts, very often in two solid colors, which is what I did in "Cymru Am Byth," on p. 13. Called "strippies," they are quite similar to old Amish "bars" quilts. They're very simple to cut and sew; but, unlike the symmetry of their Amish counterparts, the strips are often lavishly quilted with a different design for each band, as you can see in my quilts on p. 13 and below. There is an example of a wide-strip design on p. 16; I give step-by-step directions for making your own design on the facing page.

Least seen of the quilted areas, *narrow borders* (which hung over the edge of the bed) were often very simple. One from the Welsh medallion quilt in the Victoria and Albert Museum, London, is drawn on p. 16; I used it on "Cymru Am Byth."

Individual quilting designs that might be part of an overall patchwork quilt top, as in the quilt shown on p. 12, or of a medallion border, were often triangular, as shown on p. 16. In "Owain Glyndŵr," I considered each shape of the top's patchwork individually. For example, all the 3-in. muslin squares have a single freehand spiral; each muslin triangle that was made from two 3-in. triangles has a double spiral and leaf, also freehand; each 3-in. calico triangle has concentric

Fern, leaf, and flower vines on the white bands of "True Thomas" reflect the paths to goodness, to wickedness, and to Elfland revealed to Thomas the Rhymer.

Further reading

There is no book on making Welsh-style quilts, but the books listed here can provide useful background information.

Brittain, Judy. **The Bantam Step-By-Step Book of Needlecraft.** London and New York: Dorling Kindersley, Ltd. and Bantam Books, 1979. *Several photos of traditional Welsh quilts, some mislabeled as English.*

Morris, Jan. **The Matter of Wales.** New York: Oxford University Press, 1986. *Humorous view of Welsh culture, history.*

von Gwinner, Schnuppe. **The History of the Patchwork Quilt: Origins, Traditions and Symbols of a Textile Art.** West Chester, PA: Schiffer Publishing, Ltd., 1988. *Photograph of the only Welsh quilt at the V&A Museum in London.*

Walker, Michele. **The Complete Book of Quiltmaking.** New York: Alfred Knopf, 1986. *Photographs of a few traditional Welsh quilts, some Welsh quilt lore.*

Working with half-circle templates

To mark all my quilts, I use a sharp No. 3 hard pencil, or a sharp Berol Veri-thin pencil in silver or white. These lines will wash out in the first or second washing of the quilt. To make templates, which are much easier to use than cups and saucers, I use rulers, compass, scissors, paper, and template material.

Follow the five steps in the drawing at top left, facing page, to cut a half-circle template. Here's how to make a template fit the space you have in mind:

Templates for borders

If you want the **width** completely filled, the template's radius should equal the width of the strip or border. If there is a seam allowance you don't want to stitch through, make the template's radius at least ¼ in. less than the border width.

If you want the design to fill the **length** of a border or strip completely and symmetrically, cut the template so that the radius is a multiple of the strip's length (i.e., length of border divided by radius equals a whole number).

To make a template that perfectly accommodates **both the width and the length of the borders**, test several acceptable radii to see if you can find one that fits the width and is also a multiple of both border lengths. For example, if your borders are 6 in. wide and 54 in. and 60 in. long, templates with a 3-in., 2-in., or 1½-in. radius will work. You may not always be so lucky. You may need to compromise. Most often the Welsh quilters let the design run off at the ends so it would fill the width perfectly.

The step-by-step drawings opposite show how I marked the border on "Owain Glyndŵr."

Templates for squares

If you want the circular design to **fill the square** edge to edge, make the diameter of template equal one side of square.

If you wish to avoid seams or to **leave space around the edges of the square,** subtract at least ½ in. from the template's diameter to allow for the ¼-in. seam allowances around the square. If you make the design smaller than the square, be sure to mark a cross lightly inside the square to locate the exact center and the midpoints of the sides to use for reference when marking. Always do your marking from the center of the square outward. – M. W.

How to draw a half-circle template

1. Mark a straight edge on template material. Don't trust the existing edge.

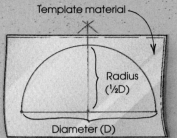

Template material

Radius (½D)

Diameter (D)

2. Mark ends (diameter) and midpoint (one end of radius) on the line.

3. Put compass needle on midpoint with lead touching one end point. Draw arc to other end.

4. Open compass. Mark short arcs above half circle by placing needle at each end point. Draw radius by connecting intersection of arcs and midpoint.

5. Cut out template and label it by size of radius, diameter, or both.

Step-by-step "Welsh Leaves Border"

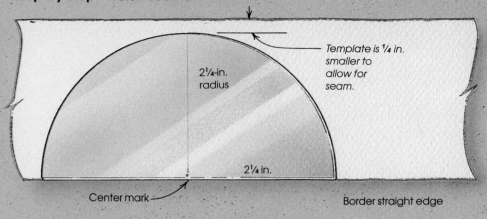

Template is ¼ in. smaller to allow for seam.

2¼-in. radius

2¼ in.

Center mark

Border straight edge

1. Mark center of border and straight edge of border (if necessary).

2. Align radius of template with center mark on border and set diameter on border edge. Draw around curve.

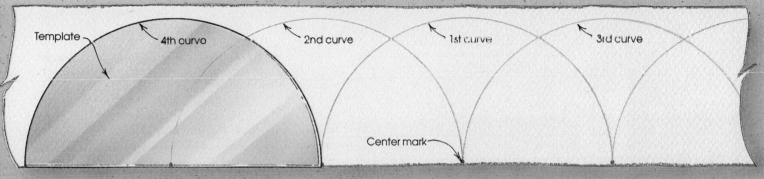

Template

4th curve

2nd curve

1st curve

3rd curve

Center mark

3. Align edge of template with center mark for 2nd and 3rd curves, one on either side of center.

4. Align template center with outer edge of 2nd and 3rd curves to draw next curves on either side, and so on to ends of border.

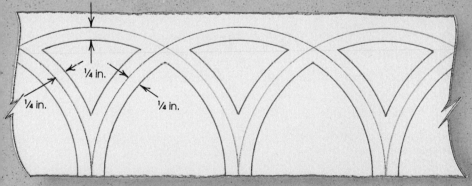

¼ in.

¼ in.

¼ in.

5. Freehand outline upper and lower shapes on insides of curves.

6. Mark leaf center veins, then use 90° corner to mark additional veins starting at leaf-tops.

90°

7. Fill in top shapes with spirals (if small), three-part leaf design, or combination, as desired.

Other fill-ins

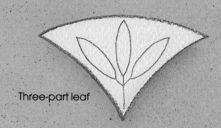

Three-part leaf

Big and little spirals

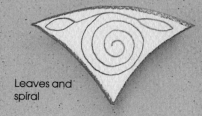

Leaves and spiral

Illustration by Clarke

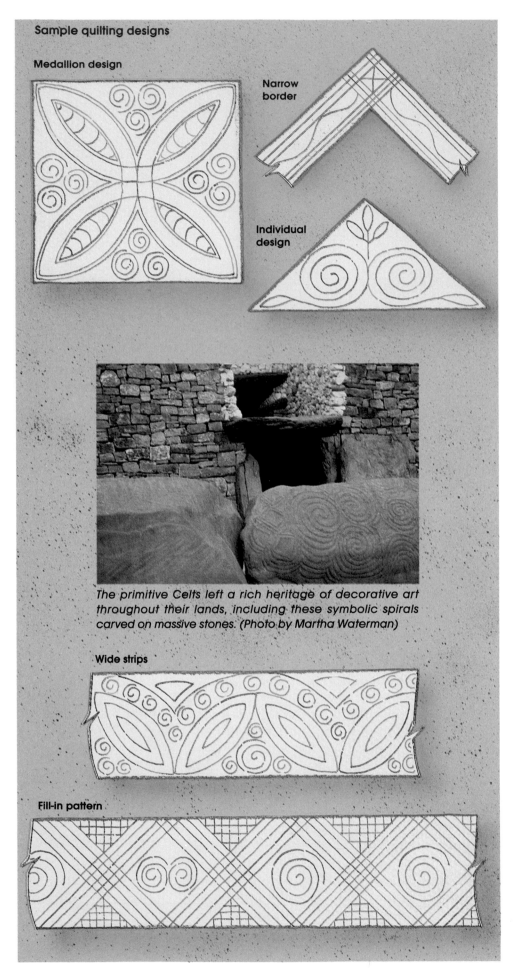

Sample quilting designs

Medallion design

Narrow border

Individual design

The primitive Celts left a rich heritage of decorative art throughout their lands, including these symbolic spirals carved on massive stones. (Photo by Martha Waterman)

Wide strips

Fill-in pattern

freehand arcs; and so on.

Even when the patchwork is angular, curved lines are prominent in the quilting. The three-part design on the triangle at left is a frequent element of Celtic art related to the three-branched motif called a triskele so common in illuminated manuscripts. A similar design is also found on Egyptian and Mycenaean scepters, where they are known as trisulas—three-pointed, tridentlike emblems.

Spirals were often used to fill in squares in Welsh quilts. They must be done freehand, but they are not difficult if you start in the center and quilt outward. When I discovered it is much easier to *quilt* them than to draw them, I quit marking them altogether.

Fill-in patterns are any quilter's stock-in-trade, and Welsh patterns are many and various. Most have curved lines and are based on the circle, but cross-hatch diamonds are also frequently seen on antique Welsh quilts, especially when combined with spirals.

Many of the patterns I saw on old Welsh quilts were clearly drawn freehand, and the quiltmaker often saw fit to include the odd variation, as in the example at bottom left. On "True Thomas," I filled the striped squares with Thomas's harp and the four-patch squares with shamrock wreaths cut from folded paper. (Shamrocks traditionally mark the places on earth that are close to the otherworld.) But one of the four-patch squares is a bit different; I filled it with a free-hand spiderweb. Such an exuberant, devil-may-care attitude is particularly Celtic in nature and is apt to be condemned as "careless work" by those who come from more stoic backgrounds. But breaking out of rigid conventions in this way is a lot of fun.

There is no English word that can convey the meaning of the Welsh word *hwyl*, a fiery and passionate exuberance; a fierce joy; a deep-rooted, forward-moving emotional force. Perhaps it is what Dylan Thomas had in mind in his poem "The Force that Through the Green Fuse Drives the Flower." Welsh quilting has *hwyl* in every hairpin turn, every breakneck curve, in the wild variety and complexity of the designs. Careless work only good enough for everyday use? No one with a shred of *hwyl* could think so! □

Martha Waterman, of Finchford, IA, teaches, writes about, and creates traditional needlework, particularly needlework of Ireland, Scotland, and Wales. Her book, Traditional Knitted Shawls, *will be published by Dos Tejedoras in the summer of 1992.*

Patterns in Motion

Shifting the design off center enlivens the traditional quilt block

by Lenore Parham

What happens when you offset a traditional quilt block? Quilt maker Mary Ann Rush asked herself this question about the traditional pineapple pattern (shown on p. 18), which consists of a series of narrow strips around a central square. By moving the center of the pattern off to one side, Mary Ann discovered that the once-predictable block suddenly became unfamiliar. The resulting asymmetry produces a potentially more interesting and naturally more active design. Fascinating and often unpredictable overall patterns emerge when the individual blocks are put together, particularly when they're constructed with strongly contrasting light and dark prints that also vary in visual texture, as shown in Mary Ann's quilts above and on p. 20.

First, I'll explain how Mary Ann and I draft her offset block. You can use this concept to redraft almost any traditional quilt block in whatever size, degree of offset, and proportional variation you desire. The next step is to experiment with various light and dark color placements by shading drawings of the draft. And finally, I'll explain the sewing technique that we use to make a complex block surprisingly easy to sew accurately.

Drafting the design

In my example, the strips on one side of the block are twice the width of those on the other side. A two-to-one ratio is easy to work with, and the results are visually satisfying. Blocks whose dimensions are a multiple of 3 in. lend themselves easily to this proportion. Those that are a multiple of 5 in. might work more logically at a three-to-two ratio. Experiment with whatever ratio of offset pleases you. ⇨

When you group asymmetrical blocks, a sense of motion results, particularly if you follow the author's suggestions for planning light and dark placement. Mary Ann Rush's quilt "Implosion" gets its name from the dark corner intersections.

From *Threads* magazine (May 1993) 46:65-69

Drafting an offset quilt block

To draft any asymmetrical block, you must establish a new "center" by relocating the horizontal, vertical, and diagonal intersection point and dividing these three axes into equal increments as shown in the steps below. Any amount of offset is possible, and you may even decide to vary the increments. These instructions are based on a 3-in. square.

Traditional pineapple block

The traditional pineapple is composed of four concentric squares whose corners have been removed to give the appearance of a square on point surrounded by narrow strips.

1 Outline a 3-in. square (the block). Draw a vertical line 1 in. in from left edge. Draw a horizontal line 1 in. up from bottom. The intersection is new center of block.

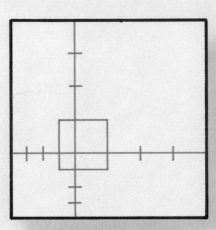

2 Working from intersection out, divide each line into four equal parts. (Spacings will be ½ in. on lines above and to right of center and ¼ in. below and to left of center.)

3 Connect first set of four marks nearest intersection to form center square (left).

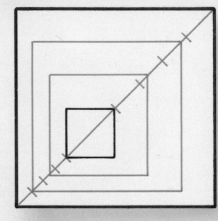

4 Connect remaining sets of marks to form outer squares.

5 Erase original dividing lines.

6 Draw diagonal line from lower left corner to upper right corner.

7 Starting from upper right corner of center square, place four marks at ½-in. intervals along diagonal line. The last division will be slightly oversized (above). Starting from lower left corner of center square, place four marks at ¼-in. intervals along diagonal line. Again, the last space will be slightly larger.

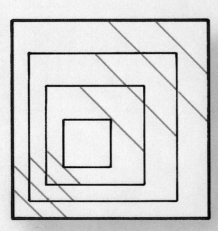

8 Extend lines to edges of squares.

9 Erase original diagonal line and encroaching corners.

10 Shade in areas as shown.

11 To form acute triangular "wings" that will add a sense of motion, draw lines connecting shaded areas and just touching corners of center square.

12 Draw remaining lines parallel to first wings.

13 Shade in wings.

For your final pattern draft and foundation, do not shade the sections.

Illustration by Clarke

Mary Ann and I work in miniature with 3-in. blocks, but you can try our sample draft in any scale. You'll need graph paper scaled eight squares to the inch, a small transparent quilters' ruler, a pencil, and a good eraser. Then follow the steps in the drawing on the facing page.

Experimenting with light and dark

Before you even look at fabric, shade in copies of your draft with a fine-point black marker, as shown at right. By working in black and white first, without the distraction of color, it is easier to concentrate on the shape of the block design and its potential. Try as many ideas as you can. You may also want to introduce medium values by shading some areas less densely.

Using a foundation for accurate sewing

Reproduce your draft exactly on a foundation that you can see through, such as muslin, tracing paper, or any of the new tear-away stabilizers. You'll sew each block from the center outward by placing pre-cut strips on the unmarked side of the foundation, right

With one block sewn, see how four will look when joined by placing the block between two mirrors taped at a right angle. Rotate the block to see remarkably different sets. Use the same technique to try shading and quilting patterns.

Shading diagram

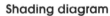

Shade different areas of your draft with black marker to experiment with light and dark placement. Add gray tone for a third intensity.

sides together, and sewing along the lines on the marked side of the foundation. Strips need not be cut precisely but must be large enough to allow plenty of seam allowance. Finger-press each strip after it has been sewn and trim the seam allowance before placing and sewing the next strip. All points "match" perfectly with almost no effort. Our foundations are stamped with numbers that indicate sewing sequence as well, as you can see on p. 20.

Both tracing paper and the tear-aways can be removed after sewing to lessen bulk for easier quilting. Mary Ann machine pieces and hand quilts. I enjoy handsewing on muslin for a stable backing, espe-

cially when I don't plan to use quilting or batting.

To make your foundation, use a square of tracing paper or muslin 1 in. larger than your sample block (4-in. foundation for a 3-in. block). Tape it over the full-size pattern you've drafted and trace carefully, using a ruler and a fine-point permanent marker.

If you decide you like this technique and want to make many blocks, marking foundations this way can be very tedious. Instead, Mary Ann had a rubber stamp made of her design (stamp available from Quilt Arts, 4114 Minstrell La., Fairfax, VA 22033). Most print shops and many office supply stores will make a stamp for you of your own

design. With the stamp, be sure to use a *permanent* ink. We use Carter's Neat-flo Stamp Pad Inker and a 4½- by 7¼-in. uninked stamp pad. (Both are available in most office supply or stationery stores). Instead of a rubber stamp, you could also try using heat-transfer pencils or smudgeless transfer paper, such as Saral from Dritz. Whatever you use, the imprint must show through to the other side. And if your foundations are muslin, the marks must be permanent through washing.

Cutting the fabric—You can use as few as two or three fabrics or as many as twenty-seven in a single offset pineapple block. (See "Working with prints" on p. 20.) I recommend starting out with four or five: a dark theme fabric, another dark or medium value print in a color found in the theme fabric, one or two background prints in a very light value of a color in the theme fabric, and an accent or bright color for the wings.

For your practice piece, try putting the theme fabric in the center square as well as the wide, dark-shaded areas. Place

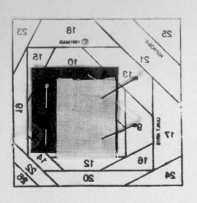

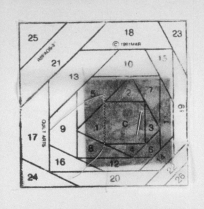

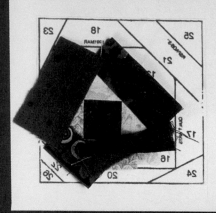

Sewing from the center out on a marked foundation: *Place the center piece right side out on the wrong side of the foundation, making sure all four sides extend generously beyond the center square. Then place piece 1 on the center, right sides together. To ensure proper placement, stab locator pins through the ends of the sewing line (left). Turn the foundation over and remove the locator pins (make sure the pin holding the center is out of the way of your presser foot). Sew along line 1, beginning* *and ending just beyond the line (center).*

Turn the block over and make sure the strip is sewn correctly. Then use your nail to finger-press the piece right side out, and trim the seam allowance to a scant ¼ in. Continue placing then sewing, pressing, and trimming each piece in order. Since each seam extends a little beyond its line, the next seam will overlap it, so you don't need to backstitch. Piece 8 has been sewn (right) and every corner looks sharp and precise.

Working with prints

Most quilters collect fabrics in color ranges, but for effective contrast when working with prints, you must also think in terms of scale (size) and texture (intensity, depth, and variety of imagery).

Take a close look at your fabric collection. How much variety do you really have? If you collect mostly traditional calicos, you already have an abundance of regularly repeating small-scale textures. But for a dynamic block, it is important to vary the scale and visual texture of the prints you plan to use, the perfect excuse to expand your fabric collection.

To preview a fabric, cut slits the width of the strips in an unruled 3-by 5-in. card . Move the card over the fabric to get an idea of what the fabric will look like in the block.

Texture—In addition to the usual florals and foliage, look for spirals, dots, plaids, checks, abstracts, and geometrics, as well as fabrics that look like stones, feathers, water, or sky. Buy prints in scales ranging from little to large. You can choose certain areas to use, or cut at random to exploit the unexpected.

Scale—Usually the smallest scale prints go in the narrowest strips, the larger ones in the wider strips. But instead of using all one color or fabric on a particular side of your block, try either several values of the same color or the same value but different textures or scales.

Contrast—The eye is attracted to areas of greatest contrast. So if you want a dark center square to stand out, the fabrics immediately surrounding it should be light. And to retain contrast between light and dark areas, choose background fabrics that support your main fabric rather than compete with it. Cut narrow strips on grain to increase their stability. Plaids, however, can be especially effective cut on the bias. And notice how stripes pull each group of four blocks together in the quilt at left.

Getting started—Quilt artist Mary Ann Rush often starts with a large-scale multicolor print—I call it a theme fabric—and decides where she will use it in the block. For example, in her quilt shown at left, the theme fabric is a rosy, marbled print that appears in the center square and the acute right triangles of most, but not all, of the blocks. She then picks coordinating prints in several shades of the colors in the

You can use both light and dark fabrics to pull a design together as well as to provide a strong contrast in a composition of various-scale prints. Another trick that artist Marilyn Rush uses in "Steel Drums" is to place the same type and scale of fabric in the same positions in each of her nine 4-block units.

the other dark or medium fabric in the narrow dark areas. Use one background fabric for all the light strips, or use two fabrics—one for the wide areas and the other for the narrow areas.

A rotary cutter, mat, and transparent quilters' ruler make quick and accurate strips, squares, and triangles. Cut your strips on grain, making sure that they are *at least* ½ in. wider than the widest area each is intended to cover on the foundation. Then cut the strips to their approximate individual lengths by laying them against the full-size pattern and adding a generous ¼ in. on either end. Use your shading diagram and the pattern to cut and arrange the pieces in order, and use both for reference when sewing.

Sewing sequence—Years ago, Lesly Claire Greenberg of Quilt Arts, in Fairfax, VA, taught us her sewing technique. The sewing is done on the marked side of the foundation so that you can see the stitching lines, and the fabric is placed on the other side. This may seem rather awkward at first, but the result will be perfect sewing accuracy without precise cutting of individual pieces, a real boon when you are dealing with a lot of tiny pieces and narrow seams.

Whether you sew by hand or machine, use small stitches just big enough for your seam ripper. Backstitching with the sewing machine is not necessary since the stitching lines are always crossed with a new line. Just start a stitch or so before the line and end a stitch after. When handsewing, secure your starting and ending stitches with a knot or a backstitch. For machine work, I recommend using a fine cotton thread such as Mettler 100 percent cotton embroidery thread. For handsewing, use cotton thread and the same needle that you use for hand piecing. I use a No. 10 or 12 between needle and No. 40 or 50 thread. Choose a neutral thread color.

Begin by placing the center square on the unmarked side of the foundation, right side out. Hold it up to the light to see that you've allowed adequate seam allowance all around. Now you sew the pieces from the center out in numerical order, as shown in the top photo on the facing page. When you are sewing pieces this small, you use pins only to guide placement, not to hold the fabric in place for sewing.

When the sewing is complete, press the block. Using a quilters' transparent ruler, add a ¼-in. seam allowance all around the outside edge and trim. When sewing blocks together, use pins to keep them lined up, and press seams open to reduce bulk. ☐

Lenore Parham, from Vienna, VA, teaches workshops at the annual Jinny Beyer Quilting Seminar, Hilton Head, SC. Mary Ann Rush's quilts will be on display at G Street Fabrics (11854 Rockville Pike, Rockville, MD 20852; 301-231-8998) until Mar. 25.

theme fabric. A bright, highly contrasting accent fabric fills out her palette.

For your first offset pineapple block, start out by choosing your theme fabric, a bold or wild large print without much white or solid-colored area. This will be the starting point for the rest of your fabric choices. Usually, ¼ yd. of theme fabric is sufficient to make a piece with 16 three-in.-blocks and a border; you'll need lesser amounts of the supporting fabrics.

Sharpening up the effect—If your block looks dull or boring, check to see that you have enough contrast between light and dark areas and that your accent is really a brighter value than anything else so that it stands out. Finally, make sure that you have enough textural variety so that the fabrics don't all look alike. Lack of contrast is often the culprit. Try making a photocopy of the block or the fabrics you're considering, as shown at far right, to help you determine the problem. Eliminating the distraction of color is one of the best ways to evaluate scale, texture, and contrast.—L.P.

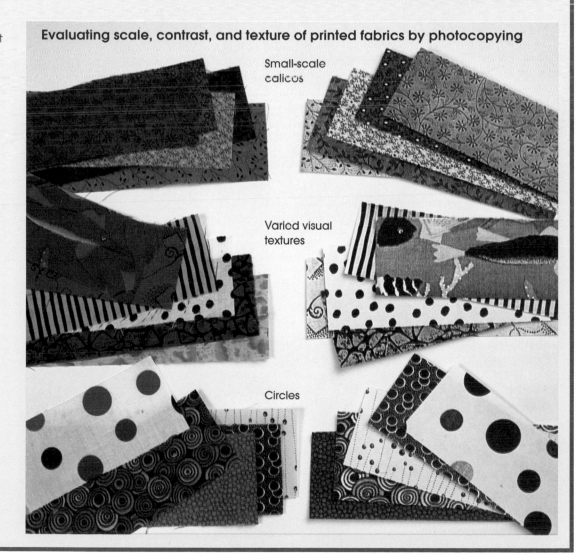

Evaluating scale, contrast, and texture of printed fabrics by photocopying

Small-scale calicos

Varied visual textures

Circles

Piecing Perfect Points

Do it with invisible hand appliqué

by Ami Simms

From *Threads* magazine (March 1992) 39:46-49

i'm convinced that there are only two stitches quiltmakers need to master: the running or quilting stitch to join the fabric sandwich together, and invisible appliqué to join the pieces. Most quilters would agree with me about the former stitch, but few would agree about the latter—until they've tried it.

The vast majority of quilters tend to shy away from traditional appliqué because it's hard to do well without a substantial time investment. Even then, many achieve only limited success. After hours of practice, sustained effort, and the gnashing of teeth, the thread "just shows a little." Swell. Most figure it wasn't worth the pain and vow to pick a pieced pattern next time.

But there's an easier way to appliqué, which gives great results with very little effort. It actually makes appliqué fun, and it's not intimidating. I call it "invisible appliqué," but it's just a simple ladder stitch as shown in the lower photo, p. 24. Best of all, it's incredibly versatile. It can be used on any project that requires appliqué—and plenty that don't. Use it for sewing traditional layered-block appliqué, reverse appliqué, needle-turn appliqué, Baltimore-album-style appliqué, pictorial quilts, stained glass technique, Celtic, and lots more. And you can even (gasp!) piece with it, as shown on the facing page.

Invisible appliqué is ideal for piecing blocks with many sharp points, like Ami Simm's "Carpenter's Wheel." Since you're always sewing on the RS from point to point, you can't have any nasty surprises when you join the last seam. And seam allowances can't pile up and distort an otherwise perfect block. (Photo by S. Kahn)

What makes invisible appliqué different?

Traditional appliqué involves some preparation before one can begin stitching. Sewing lines must be marked, and the seam allowances must be trimmed and tucked under. Some folks just press them under; others baste. Some fuse them to freezer paper; others stitch them to templates. I would not be surprised if the next fad involves a hot glue gun. With invisible appliqué, the preparation is much simpler. Mark sewing lines on both the piece to be appliquéd and the background. Trim the seam allowance of the appliqué piece to ¼ in. (⅛ in. if you're working on tight curves, sharp points, or very small pieces), and begin.

In traditional appliqué, the needle moves at an angle. The object is to take minuscule bites out of both pieces of fabric with the same stitch. The smaller the bite, the less the thread shows. Because the needle moves at an angle, the seam allowance is caught with every stitch and held in place.

With invisible appliqué, the needle moves straight along the sewing lines, first taking a chunk out of one piece of fabric, then out of the other—never both at the same time. As long as the needle is inserted precisely opposite where the thread from the last stitch exits, the thread will never show. Not at all. Also, because the needle goes in on the sewing line and comes out on the sewing line, you never catch the seam allowance. This is why you can use invisible appliqué for more than just appliqué.

How do you do it?

It's important to keep the grainlines in the appliqué piece and the background consistent to ensure predictable sewing.

Both pieces of cloth will either stretch or not stretch to the same degree. It's never any fun trying to sew bias to straight grain. One moves and the other doesn't. Keeping grainlines straight also helps keep colors consistent, especially when you're working with solids. Lengthwise grain also contributes to sounder construction and therefore better appearance, so I recommend it in most cases. Sometimes, however, the fabric's pattern or your design scheme will be inconsistent with maintaining vertical grain. If that is the case, go with the fabric or your own taste.

To practice the stitch, cut out a square template. Align the template the same way relative to the grain on both the background and appliqué pieces of fabric, and mark around it on the right side of both pieces of fabric. Keep the marking lines as thin and accurate as possible, and make sure that the corners are fully drawn and sharp. If the appliqué looks symmetrical but isn't, put an orientation mark on one side of the template and mark that side in the seam allowance of both pieces so you'll be able to orient the appliqué consistently, as shown in the left-hand drawing below. Trim the seam allowance around the appliqué piece to ¼ in. just before you're ready to sew it. Don't clip corners and don't fold, press, or baste the seam allowance under.

You always sew from the right side, and the seam you're sewing is always at the top. Now look at the drawings below. Place the appliqué on top of the background with the seam you're about to sew at the top, and slide the appliqué down so both seamlines show. Thread your favorite size needle with about a 12-in. piece of contrasting hand sewing thread, and knot the end. Polyester-

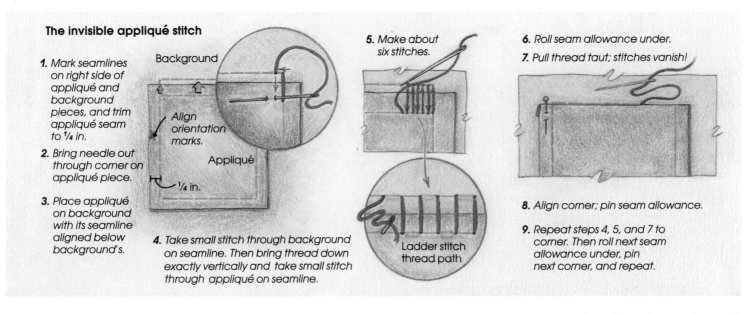

The invisible appliqué stitch

Background

Align orientation marks.

Appliqué

¼ in.

1. Mark seamlines on right side of appliqué and background pieces, and trim appliqué seam to ¼ in.

2. Bring needle out through corner on appliqué piece.

3. Place appliqué on background with its seamline aligned below background's.

4. Take small stitch through background on seamline. Then bring thread down exactly vertically and take small stitch through appliqué on seamline.

5. Make about six stitches.

Ladder stitch thread path

6. Roll seam allowance under.

7. Pull thread taut; stitches vanish!

8. Align corner; pin seam allowance.

9. Repeat steps 4, 5, and 7 to corner. Then roll next seam allowance under, pin next corner, and repeat.

wrapped cotton is good, and you may want to wax it. Once you've mastered the stitch, choose thread that matches the appliqué piece.

Bring the needle out at the right-hand, top corner of the appliqué piece (left top, if you're left-handed). Keeping the needle parallel to and on the sewing line, take a tiny stitch in the corner of the background as shown in the detail on the left-hand drawing, p. 23. The goal is to sew about 10 stitches to the inch and to keep all the stitches the same size and the same distance apart. Bring the needle and thread through. Then bring the needle down to the appliqué exactly opposite the point where it exited the background. Take a tiny stitch in the appliqué. Bring the needle up to the background exactly opposite its last exit, and repeat. Pull the thread each time only till you've removed the slack, and be careful not to catch either the seam allowance of the appliqué or the background underneath the appliqué.

When you have six parallel vertical threads, as shown in the second drawing, p. 23, the needle will be coming out of the appliqué. Now you're ready for the magic. Use the tip of the needle or your fingers to roll the seam allowance under. Then pull the thread taut. Voilà! To make sure you haven't pulled too tight, pinch the seam between your left index finger and thumb, and slide them along the seam in the sewing direction.

Before starting the next group of stitches, line up the sewing lines at the next recognizable point, usually a corner, and pin in the seam allowance, as shown at lower right, p. 23. The pin holds everything in place and gives you a precise corner to aim for. You can remove it as you approach the corner.

When you pull the thread taut, it's very difficult to tell where the thread is coming from. (Remember, it's "invisible" appliqué.) So it's a good idea to get in the habit of always ending on the same piece. Otherwise, you're likely to skip a stitch. Also, when you pull up the thread, it draws the appliqué right to the sewing line on the background, obscuring it. Use your left thumb to nudge the piece away from the background ever so slightly so you can keep sewing right on the line. Sew another group of six or eight stitches, and pull up the thread again. Use the needle tip to roll the seam allowance under as you sew, but don't crush it flat since you need to sew just through the marked seamlines without catching fabric on either side. Use your left thumb to anchor the thread already pulled taut as you pull up the next group of stitches.

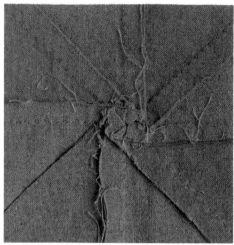

To help keep its center perfect and perfectly flat, Simms pressed all the star's seams clockwise (photo above). One of the beauties of this technique is that since the seam allowances are always kept free, you can manipulate them this way to help improve a block's appearance. Ladder stitch appliqué piecing, below, takes a little practice to perfect, but once mastered, it's as quick as the traditional methods and much more accurate.

If you're having trouble keeping the ladder stitches exactly vertical, touch the needle tip to the point where the last stitch exits the fabric before inserting the needle for the next stitch. It also helps to pull the appliqué away from the background periodically after you've drawn the thread taut. If you're sewing just right, the threads between stitches will be straight up and down, not V- or W-shaped. Check the back, too. Your stitches should be consistent, even, small, and snug enough that you can't wiggle them with your fingernail. If they're too loose, pull the thread a little tighter.

Sew right to the end of the marked line. Then gently fold under the next seam allowance, turn the work so the second side is on top, pin the far corner, and continue sewing. If the corner angle is 90 degrees or greater, you don't need to trim it. When you've sewn all four sides,

take the needle through to the wrong side of the background, catch a bit of fabric, and knot off near the stitching line.

How can you piece with ladder stitch?

Because the needle only goes through the seamline in invisible appliqué, you can move the seam allowance into any position after the seam is complete. For this reason it is ideal for making pictorial quilts. Complicated jigsaw-type patterns need not be worked by appliquéing everything to a base or "muslin." And a seam sewn with invisible appliqué is indistinguishable from a seam joined by traditional hand piecing. For simplicity's sake, give it a try following the directions for stitching a nine-patch (see the drawings on the facing page).

You don't need orientation marks for piecing, but grainline is very important. I always make a piecing diagram and mark vertical grainline on every single patch, as shown at top left, facing page. Then I lay out my fabric with the grainline running vertically and mark my pieces with the template(s). Leave more than the standard ¼-in. seam allowance because with appliqué piecing, some seam allowances will need to be larger. When you've cut out the patches, mark grain arrows on one seam allowance of each. Then lay the patches out right sides up with grainlines vertical according to the piecing diagram, center left, opposite.

Usually, you want to join the patches with the seam allowances folded under the dark patches. If you treat the dark patches as the appliqué pieces, this will happen automatically. Sewing order in appliqué piecing is the same as in traditional hand piecing. Use the same strategy that you would if you were joining patches on the machine or by hand using a running stitch. The seam allowances can be pressed wherever you want them to go *after the fact*. If you stick with the "dark on top" strategy, you just won't have to reposition seam allowances, as they will be finger pressed as you sew under the dark patch. Similarly, sew dark strips to light strips as shown in the lower left drawing, facing page.

Trim the first seam allowance of the first dark piece and sew it to the adjacent light piece just as you would for an invisible appliqué seam. Knot off at the end of the seamline, and trim the seam allowance of the light piece. Then trim and sew the next dark piece to the other side of the light piece, as shown at top right, opposite, and trim it. When you've assembled three strips, sew the predominantly dark strips to the predominantly

Appliqué piecing a nine-patch

Piecing diagram

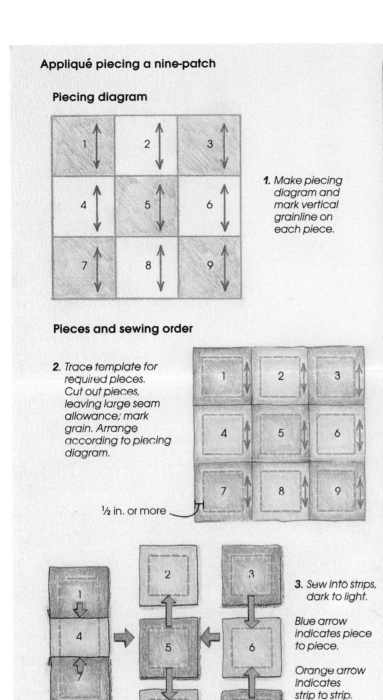

1. Make piecing diagram and mark vertical grainline on each piece.

Pieces and sewing order

2. Trace template for required pieces. Cut out pieces, leaving large seam allowance; mark grain. Arrange according to piecing diagram.

½ in. or more

3. Sew into strips, dark to light.

Blue arrow indicates piece to piece.

Orange arrow indicates strip to strip.

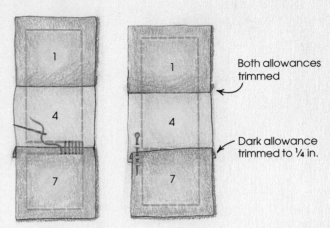

Both allowances trimmed

Dark allowance trimmed to ¼ in.

4. Trim seam allowance on first dark piece's first seam (1). Always sew dark to light; sew 1 to 4. Knot off at end of seam, and trim seam allowance on 4. Repeat for 7 to 4. Next sew 5 to 2, then 5 to 8. Finally sew 3 to 6 and 9 to 6.

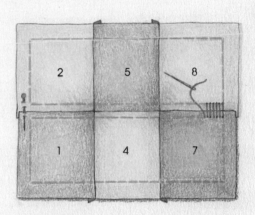

5. Sew dark strip, 1-4-7, to light strip, 2-5-8; then remaining dark strip, 3-6-9, to other side of light strip. Keep seam allowances free at corners. Trim each appliqué strip's seam allowance just before sewing seam and each background's seam allowance just after.

Illustrations by Christine Charbonneau

light strip, as shown at lower right. Since the seam allowances are all under the dark patches, which makes them a little higher, and since dark and light patches alternate, the corners will fit together perfectly. Pin beyond the corner in the seam allowance.

Why is invisible piecing better?

The advantages of using invisible appliqué to hand piece are twofold: First, since the stitching is done from the right side, you'll be able to see if your points meet precisely as you sew them, not after you've knotted off, flipped your work over, and opened it up. Second, you no longer have to avoid patterns with set-in patches. They are simply appliquéd now, as are the rest of the patches, and nobody will ever be the wiser. When the seam is finished, there is no way to tell hand-pieced blocks from hand-appliquéd blocks, except that the hand-appliquéd blocks might be better.

It may also be argued that no one in her right mind would hand stitch a nine-patch. I agree; life is too short. I presented it here merely as an instructional vehicle to introduce you to invisible appliqué piecing. □

Ami Simms expanded on the full range of this technique's possibilities in her book Invisible Applique *(Mallery Press, 1988). Parts of this article are drawn from it. For a copy, send $9.95 plus $1.50 S&H (4% sales tax for MI residents) to Mallery Press, Dept. T, 4206 Sheraton Dr., Flint, MI 48532. Autographs on request.*

A Vest for Quilters

Flattering shape, a thin batt, and a clean finish

by Rachel Kincy Clark

Planning a Japanese vest, author Rachel Clark arranges strips of fabric selected from her collection. Having chosen a theme and a palette of fabrics, she lets her creativity fill in her vest design. Her original pattern for the vest is shown on the facing page.

my garments make statements. They tell stories, they reflect my passions, my history, and, I hope, my sense of humor. My clothes are for women who have a sure sense of themselves, who know their own minds and aren't afraid to show it.

Statements, however, are not my only concern. Materials, fit, and construction are critical as well. There is no point in making a statement if the garment falls apart the first time it is worn or cleaned. Finally, I consider the sheer beauty of the piece. I want the wearer to say "Wow!" every time she puts it on.

My mask vest series began when I read *African Masks* by Robert Beakley. First one mask, then another, called out to me to be interpreted into fiber until I'd done seven vests with mask themes.

I'm not sure where I would have gone next, but a friend made a change in my direction by commissioning a piece based on her Scandinavian heritage. I spent some time studying Scandinavia before I began sketching. I based the piecing of the vest front on Norwegian cross-stitch patterns and took the quilting motifs from Norse artifacts. I included Thor's hammer, Viking spears, and the crosses I found on the sides of ships. The colors were primarily the cool blues, greens, and magentas I associated with the far north.

After Africa and Europe, my next stop was Asia. I have always loved the beauty and subtlety of Japanese design, so I looked for and adapted motifs from traditional and contemporary Japanese sources. The result is the vest shown in the photo at right on the facing page.

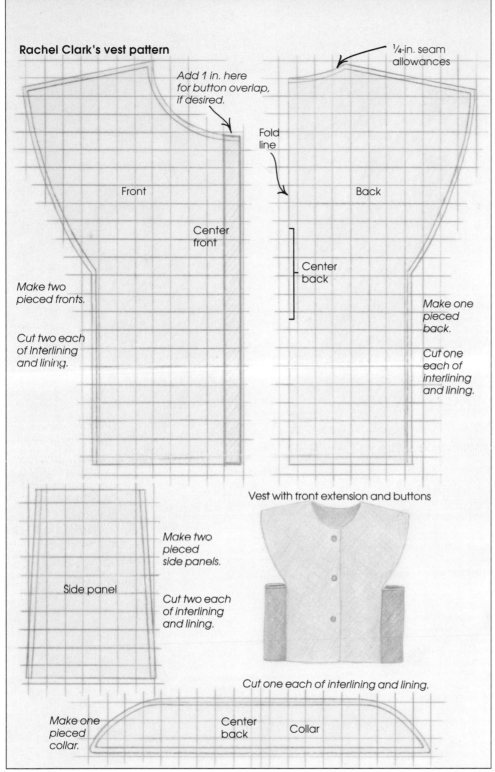

Rachel Clark's vest pattern

¼-in. seam allowances

Add 1 in. here for button overlap, if desired.

Fold line

Front

Back

Center front

Center back

Make two pieced fronts.

Cut two each of Interlining and lining.

Make one pieced back.

Cut one each of interlining and lining.

Vest with front extension and buttons

Side panel

Make two pieced side panels.

Cut two each of interlining and lining.

Cut one each of interlining and lining.

Make one pieced collar.

Center back

Collar

Beads and baubles decorate Rachel Clark's Asian vest. The right front includes a panel of pieced higake (braided fence). The upper part of the left front is strip-pieced on a diagonal, and appliquéd pine bark diamonds on the lower left front appear to float one above the other. Clark chose stylized gingko leaves as the quilting motif. (Photo by Susan Kahn)

Collecting materials

My techniques depend on having a very large collection of fabrics, threads, ribbons, buttons, and beads. I have collected such things for years because it is just not possible to go out and buy everything I need for a garment at one time. Japanese ikats, batiks, and silk brocades are a sheer joy to work with. Many come from recycled kimono, and others are available in 14-in.-wide yardage. While not inexpensive, Japanese fabrics are certainly worth the extra cost.

Unique fabrics can often be salvaged from damaged antique linens and garments. Old buttons, beads, and coins are especially nice. It's also useful that I have a large circle of friends who are generous enough to run their cast-off clothing and costume jewelry past me. Broken jewelry often has parts that can be salvaged into wonderful touches.

I have strong feelings about linings. I generally use several different fabrics and some piecing. Of course this allows me to use scraps, but the primary purpose is to insure the artistic integrity of the entire piece. Even though the lining is usually seen only by the person wearing the garment, I want her to know that every detail mattered.

A versatile vest pattern

My pattern, shown at left above, fits a size 10 or a flat-chested 12, but you can easily adapt the pattern to your figure. Most adjustments to the bust or hips can be made on the side section. Be sure to allow for wearing ease. Add one inch to the center of the fronts if you want an extension for buttons and buttonholes.

After researching and sketching my

ideas, I choose bits from the different sketches to complete my design. I cut out the vest pattern, including ¼-inch seam allowances, from "examination table" paper. Pattern-making paper works, also. I transfer my final design to the pattern. If I need templates to cut precise shapes for piecing the design, I can cut them from this copy. If the design calls for random pieces, the copy is my guide. If I have more ideas than I'm willing to give up, I sometimes make a reversible vest.

Finding the right fabric—All my mask vests have a geographic or ethnic theme which I reinforce with fabrics that come from that country or region, or are related to it by pattern designs in the cloth. I prefer natural fibers, but I am not wedded to them. If the color, texture, quality, and pattern are appropriate, I will use synthetics. When I combine fabrics, I keep in mind how they will be laundered. I feel it is inappropriate to make a garment using all washable fabric, then add a "dry-clean only" fabric.

I take piles of fabric from my stash, matching them until I'm happy with my choices. I usually work with a large palette of fabrics—as many as 18. The fabric I choose at this step defines the boundaries in which I work. I may use pieces differently than I'd originally planned, but I don't add more possibilities later. I can then make my fronts, sides, and back separately, confident that because of my earlier selections, the finished vest will hang together as a cohesive unit.

Add-ons—I go through my embellishments, selecting what I will need to enhance my vest. I include beads, buttons, bells, baubles, quilting patterns, appliqués, stenciling, or other fabric decoration techniques that are compatible.

Constructing the vest fabric

I make my vests from pieced, appliquéd, and embellished fabric that is attached to a muslin or flannel interlining as it is made. This stabilizes the fabric, improves the shape of the vest, and eliminates stretching and sagging. Each garment piece (front, side back, collar) is made separately, then the completed pieces are sewn together to complete the vest. Sometimes I use batting in special areas that I want accented, but never for the full vest because I don't like the puffy, overstuffed look that I get.

Piecing—I find it easiest to cut out the interlining and, using the design on my paper pattern as a guide, work out the final placement of pieced fabrics directly on it, as I'm doing in the photo on p. 26. The *hiyake*, or Braided fence, pattern near the center front in the photo has been machine pieced into a unit before attaching to the interlining. Sometimes I sew groups of fabrics together in this way before I sew them to the interlining, if I want them to appear less prominent in the design than if they were appliquéd, or if I feel that the fabrics will show to best advantage this way. To create my units, I may use miniature quilt blocks, collage, Seminole piecing techniques, or just random piecing.

I sew the pieced units to the interlining by machine, using a strip-piecing technique that incorporates single, unpieced strips into the overall design. Working from the center out, I pin a design unit, either pieced or unpieced, to the interlining, right side up. Then I pin a straight strip of contrasting or coordinating fabric to the edge, right sides together, as shown at left below. The strips I use vary in finished width from ¼ in. to 1 in. Using a ¼-in. seam allowance on the edge of the strip, I stitch through all three layers. This joins the strip to the pieced unit and to the muslin.

After each unit or strip is added, I fold the strip wrong side down and press the seam from the right side. Then I can lay the next strip on, right side down, and stitch and press in the same way.

I have a special method of piecing curved seams by machine that is a variation of this technique. I use it when I need to see exactly how two pieces will come together in the finished vest. First, I lay one piece of fabric on the interlining, right side up. Then I place the other piece right side up, with the seam allowance extending over the bottom fabric. To pin the top piece in place, I turn under the ¼-in. seam allowance and insert the point of a pin exactly into the fold as shown in the right-hand drawing below. Then I use a rocking motion to pin through the two layers of fabric under it, leaving the top fabric free. Once the seam is pinned in this way, I fold the top piece back so I can pin from the wrong side, as shown, and stitch.

After the interlining piece is covered, I use my pattern to true up the section. Sometimes during piecing and pressing, the garment piece will shrink or distort. Don't panic; just take the appropriate action. If it shrinks, add another strip. If it is too large, trim away the excess.

Hand appliqué and quilting—Appliquéd pieces add dimension to my vests. They tend to stand out from the surface and unify the design by crossing seamlines. The pine bark diamonds shown on the left vest front in the photo on p. 27 seem to be suspended above the vest's surface because they were appliquéd one over the other.

I cut out the appliqué design with a ⅛-in. to ¼-in. seam allowance. If it's a simple design, I'll just turn under the edge as I slip-stitch it invisibly onto the vest. For designs with many curves or corners, I press under the seam allowances and baste to hold them in place while I stitch. I either pin baste or thread baste all appliqués to the vest before I slip-stitch them.

If part of the appliqué will cross a garment seam, I stitch to within ½ in. of the edge and leave the applied piece dangling until after I've sewn the vest sections together. Then I slip-stitch the rest

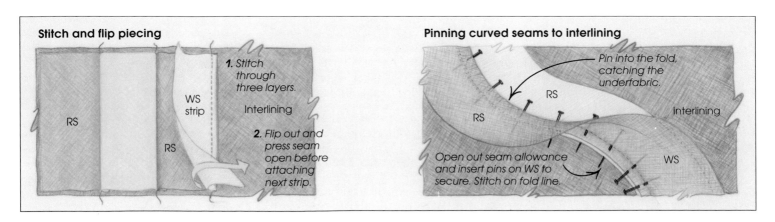

Stitch and flip piecing

RS

WS strip

RS

Interlining

1. Stitch through three layers.

2. Flip out and press seam open before attaching next strip.

Pinning curved seams to interlining

Pin into the fold, catching the underfabric.

RS

RS

Interlining

WS

Open out seam allowance and insert pins on WS to secure. Stitch on fold line.

Vest Construction

Add lining at the same time for a clean finish.

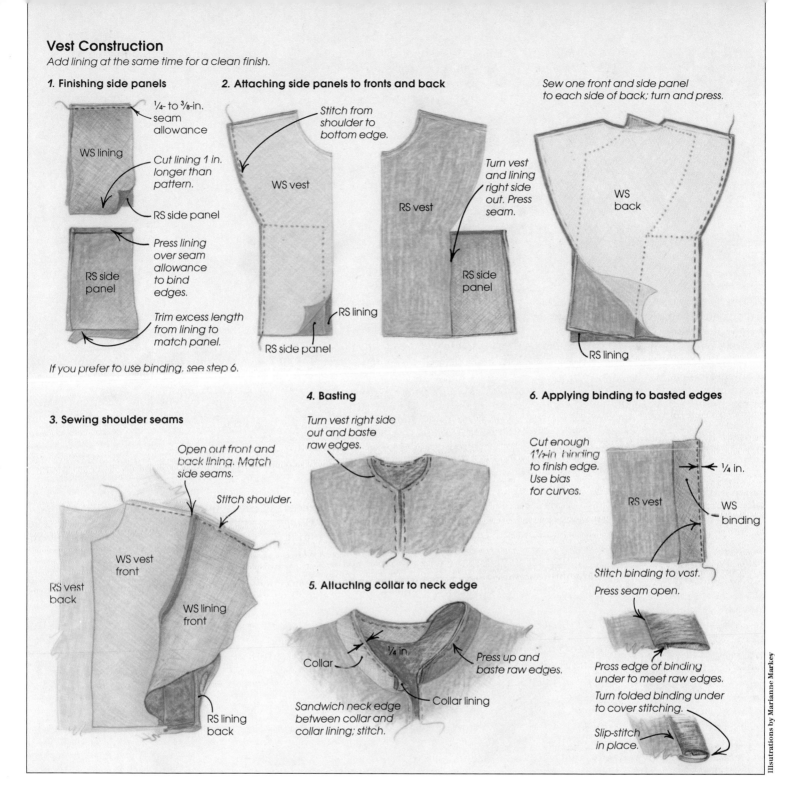

1. Finishing side panels

¼- to ⅜-in. seam allowance

WS lining

Cut lining 1 in. longer than pattern.

RS side panel

Press lining over seam allowance to bind edges.

RS side panel

Trim excess length from lining to match panel.

If you prefer to use binding, see step 6.

2. Attaching side panels to fronts and back

Stitch from shoulder to bottom edge.

WS vest

RS vest

RS lining

RS side panel

Turn vest and lining right side out. Press seam.

RS side panel

Sew one front and side panel to each side of back; turn and press.

WS back

RS lining

3. Sewing shoulder seams

Open out front and back lining. Match side seams.

Stitch shoulder.

RS vest back

WS vest front

WS lining front

RS lining back

4. Basting

Turn vest right side out and baste raw edges.

5. Attaching collar to neck edge

Collar

¼ in.

Press up and baste raw edges.

Collar lining

Sandwich neck edge between collar and collar lining; stitch.

6. Applying binding to basted edges

Cut enough 1½-in. binding to finish edge. Use bias for curves.

RS vest

¼ in.

WS binding

Stitch binding to vest.

Press seam open.

Press edge of binding under to meet raw edges.

Turn folded binding under to cover stitching.

Slip-stitch in place.

Illustrations by Marianne Markey

---

of the design to the garment.

With the piecing and appliqué complete, I work out a quilting design using motifs from the country that inspired the vest. For the Japanese vest, I chose patterns like gingko leaves and stylized waves. If quilting is not your thing, you may want to consider painting or stenciling a pattern or design to enhance the overall theme.

In addition to quilting, I sew on most of my embellishing beads, buttons, and baubles at this point because I like my lining to be loose in the garment.

Assembling the pieces

The steps in constructing the vest are shown in the drawing above. By stitching completed garment sections together, I make vests that are cleanly finished inside as well as out and can, by design, be reversible.

I cut out my lining after making the outer vest fabric because I like to use some of the same fabrics in the lining that I used in the vest. By waiting until the vest pieces are finished, I can tell what fabrics are left from the original selections and coordinate the lining to the

vest. The lining is incorporated into the vest at each assembly step.

To assemble the vest pieces, I finish the tops of the side sections, attach the fronts and backs, and then sew the shoulder seams. The last steps are to sew on the collar and bind the hem, collar, and front edges. ☐

Rachel Kincy Clark maintains her outstanding fabric hoard in Watsonville, CA, where she sews for the joy of it and teaches "Clothing for the Body and Soul" for fiber guilds and at quilting conferences.

Flowers from Baltimore Album Quilts

Tucks and gathers transform ribbon into lifelike blossoms

by Elly Sienkiewicz

ten years ago, I went to the show "Baltimore Album Quilts" at the Baltimore Museum of Art so I could lunch afterward with friends. But that casual date changed my life. The bigness, the brightness, and the timeless exuberance of those quilts enveloped me. Their effect was immediate, emotional—inexplicably they brought tears to my eyes—and compelling. And "those fascinating ladies of bygone Baltimore," as I call them, still fascinate me ten years, eight group-made album quilts, and six books on them later.

The album quilt style, collections of pictorial blocks, was a mid-nineteenth-century needlework movement that first swept the Eastern seaboard, developing distinctive regional styles around urban centers. But the album quilts from Baltimore were the most outstanding. The Baltimorean style reflected a fresh, skilled realism in draftsmanship and embellished detail and an elegant ornateness that epitomized the complex aesthetic of the Victorian era. These quilts teem with panoramic vitality. As in a photo album, life's details—momentous and mundane—are portrayed. But their dominant motif is nature's bounty and blessing: fruits, trees, stems and leaves, vines and flowers—especially flowers so lifelike that at first all you can do is marvel.

Victorian ladies all knew the symbolic meaning of flowers, and stitched them into their quilt blocks. The bouquet in the author's version below expresses gratitude, and roses, love. The realism of these flowers comes in part from the high relief made possible by shaded wire ribbon. Directions for the roses and camella in the center of the block and for the bluebells at upper left are given on the following pages.

Lately, I've become intrigued by the techniques the Baltimore album quilters used for constructing dimensional flowers. You'll find directions here for making several of the flowers shown below on my own version of a mid-nineteenth-century block from a quilt sewn by three generations of the Numsen family. I call it "Beribboned Bouquet."

Fabric for flowers

One of the first things I learned when I began to make dimensional flowers is that the weight and texture of the fabric you use is critical. Nineteenth-century flowers were made with a fine cotton most like today's poly/cotton batiste, or with silk mousselline, a fine, sheer, organza-like fabric. The important point for us to be aware of is that our normal quilt-making calicoes and broadcloths are usually too heavy.

For several years, I made flowers with tie-dyed quilters' cottons, lightweight silks, satin ribbons, and cotton/poly blends. But the French wire ribbon that has recently become widely available has been the most inspirational material of all, and it has changed my life yet again (see "Supplies" on p. 33). Not only does this *ombré*, or shaded, ribbon imitate the beauty of the shaded rainbow fabric of old

Photo by Susan Kahn

Bluebells or foxgloves

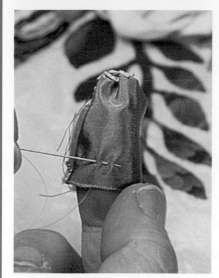

Bluebells and foxgloves are among the easiest to reproduce of the Baltimore ladies' dimensional effects. For bluebell, cut a 2-in. piece of 1-in.-wide ribbon; for foxglove, cut a 2½-in. piece of 1⅜-in.-wide ribbon. Fold it in half matching cut edges, and seam ¼ in. from raw edge. Gather top edge tightly. Then gather ¼ in. from lower edge and pull to nip in bell slightly. Set flower on background with exposed seam underneath, and push it up slightly to hide gathering at top. Push ⅓ teaspoon of poly stuffing up into cup of flower, and appliqué it to background, sewing around top half only. Finish by tucking a fringed center (described on p. 32) into the lip so it peeks out a bit, and secure by stitching from underneath. See the finished flowers on the facing page.

Seeing a room full of Baltimore album quilts, like the one on the wall behind her, sent the author on a ten-year exploration of their amazing techniques.

Baltimore with its graduated tints, but the crisp, light texture of the rayon ribbon appliqués beautifully. It also performs wonderfully in all sorts of manipulated postures because of the thin (usually copper) wire that runs through both selvages. The wire can be removed easily, but I usually leave it in.

Needle and thread

I use size 10 milliners' straw needles (from Cotton Patch) for all my appliqué work, and I like to use 100 percent nylon filament thread (the kind that is used for machine quilting) to hand stitch my flower appliqués. The nylon does not show, it's very fine, and because it's transparent, chameleon-like it takes on the color

it stitches. You finish sewing it off as usual, with three small, tight stitches on top of each other. But tying a knot in this thread is tricky. I've found that the "quilter's knot," similar to a French knot and shown in *Basics, Threads,* No. 40, p. 16, works beautifully.

Not long ago, I discovered that I can gather most straight or curved seams on my machine. I use the longest stitch length with nylon thread in the top and regular cotton or polyester sewing thread in the bobbin. The slippery nylon automatically gathers as I sew. I used this method to speed gather the 16 petals required for a puff-centered ellipse rose, as described on p. 32, backstitching at the beginning and end of each petal.

Leaves and stems

Except for the horizontal row of jagged Christmas cactus leaves in the center of my block, which were added by appliqué prepared with freezer paper inside, all the other leaves and stems were cut and sewn, a couple of inches at a time, from a square of green print. I used the "cutaway appliqué" technique: a freezer paper pattern is affixed to the right side of the fabric, and you cut out the appliqué a few inches at a time as you sew it in place. The fold line is just outside the edge of the freezer paper. (For more on this technique, refer to *Baltimore Beauties and Beyond, Volume I,* chapters 1-3, mentioned in "Further reading" on p. 33.) Using a large green print belies the fact that

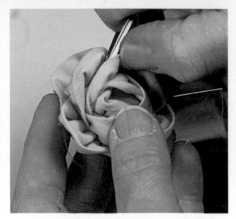

Inner petals: Using the pattern pieces shown below, hold center wrong side up and cup 1st small petal around it, aligning raw edges of center and petal. Stitch petal to center. Add 2nd petal, beginning at midpoint of 1st, overlapping clockwise. Third petal will overlap second at midpoint to cup center. Make 2nd round with remaining three small petals, overlapping each by ⅓ and keeping all raw edges on same plane.

Add larger petals in two rounds of five each. Pin beginning and end of a petal to center puff, and take additional tucks to fit it tightly. As cluster of petals around puff gets bigger, whipstitch each petal to previous layer, pulling in tiny tucks. These extra gathers tighten base and relax petal lip so rose opens and lies flatter.

Finishing: Push at center a bit to refine shape. Then turn cuffs back on certain petals, using a scissors' tip to catch lip of each petal, folding it down away from center. Tack them down if fabric won't hold crease. Finally, tack center down a bit with French knots from a single strand of cream-colored rayon Sulky embroidery floss.

Pattern for puff-centered ellipse rose

Four rounds of folded and gathered ellipse petals surround a stuffed center.

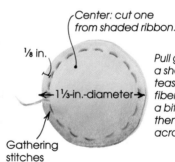

Center: cut one from shaded ribbon.

⅛ in.

1⅓-in.-diameter

Gathering stitches

Pull gathering to form a shallow cup. Stuff ¾ teaspoon of polyester fiber into it and gather a bit tighter. Backstitch then stitch loosely across filling to hold it in.

Inner petals: cut six from silk crepe.

1½-in. ellipse

2-in. ellipse

Outer petals: cut 10 from silk crepe.

Fold each petal in half lengthwise and gather slightly along curved (raw) edge by hand or machine.

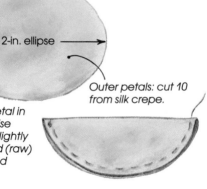

(You can find multisize templates for ellipses and circles at an art supply store.)

---

the leaves and stems are sewn from one piece and makes the block look much more complicated than it is.

Blossoms

Space prevents my giving directions for every flower on "Beribboned Bouquet," so I've concentrated on the ribbon flowers, particularly the roses, as well as on one cup-shaped flower, a bluebell or foxglove (depending on size), and one ruched blossom, a camelia. The puff-centered ellipse rose is made with a shaded ribbon center and silk or tie-dyed-cotton petals. Both the folded rolled rose and the open rolled rose are made with shaded wire ribbon, as is the camelia. The bluebell/foxglove can be made with either fabric.

Mrs. Numsen's fringed center is an excellent all-purpose center for many flowers. To make one, cut a 1¼-in.-diameter yellow circle from cotton, silk, or shaded ribbon. Fringe ½ in. of edge all around; then fold the circle into quarters and tuck the point into the flower center. A dot of glue or a tiny stitch holds it in place.

To assemble the block, pin completed blossoms in place and attach them with running stitches from behind—long underneath and short where they grab the flower, or appliqué them from the top.

The language of the flowers

Flowers were part of an expressive, symbolic language long before Victorian times, but the language was so entrenched

in Victorian culture that the meanings were immediately understood by all. Echoes of it are still familiar to us. (Everyone understands the meaning of a single red rose.) But to understand what the flowers on the quilts are saying, it's necessary to know a bit about mid-nineteenth-century sensibilities.

It was a time of public consensus with commonly held values—appreciation, community loyalty, and gratitude. The era's ideals were those same enlightenment ideals of religious tolerance, equality, and brotherhood that had shaped the United States Constitution. As I've studied the quilts together with Victorian flower language, I've come to believe that many of the quilt makers stitched flowers that affirmed their sense of who they were and what the meaning of their lives was.

Geometry—In the dimensional flowers so popular on album quilts, flowers were the medium and dimension was the message. The mathematical perfection of geometry (both plane and solid) symbolized God or moral perfection. With clear intent and great cleverness, the quilt makers showed dimension (and thus, also, realism) using shaded prints for contour, featuring lifelike prints of flowers and leaves, and manipulating fabric into the dimensional shapes of usually recognizable blossoms.

Flowers—Bouquets, like the one on the block on p. 30, symbolized gifts of love, expressions of thanks, approbation, offerings of the earth's beauty, offerings of gratitude. And daily, habitual, heartfelt expressions of gratitude were a way of life then.   ⇨

Supplies

The Cotton Patch
1025 Brown Ave.
Lafayette, CA 94549
(800) 835-4418
All books, silk wire ribbons, tie-dyed fabrics, needles; 300 swatches, $3; free catalog.

Quilters' Resource, Inc.
PO Box 148850
Chicago, IL 60614
(312) 278-5695; (800) 676-6543
All books, extensive shaded wire ribbon collection, other supplies.

Debra Lunn Fabrics
357 Santa Fe Dr.
Denver, CO 80223
(303) 623-2710
All-cotton hand-dyed fabrics; tie-dyed and gradated color fabrics, custom air brush; SASE for catalog and workshops.

Further reading

Sienkiewicz, Elly. *Baltimore Beauties and Beyond: Studies in Classic Album Quilt Appliqué, vol. I.* Martinez, CA.: C&T Publishing, 1989.
Twelve lessons in classic appliqué focus on blocks' design characteristics and construction techniques.

——. *Baltimore Beauties and Beyond: Studies in Classic Album Quilt Appliqué, vol. II.* Martinez, CA.: C&T Publishing, 1991.
Inking and picture blocks; patterns for 20 blocks and 13 borders.

——. *Spoken without a Word: A Lexicon of Selected Symbols with 24 Patterns from Classic Baltimore Album Quilts.* Washington, D.C.: Self-published, 1983.
Study of album quilt symbolism with patterns. Carried by stores listed above.

Folded rolled rose with folded ribbon leaves

1. To begin rose, gather by pulling wires on each selvage of an 18- to 20-in.-long piece of 1½-in.-wide yellow-to-fuschia shaded ribbon and fold it in half lengthwise. Fold the starting end down about 1 in. at right angle to form shank (stem below center of rose). Roll with wire edges at base, and move center wraps down shank slightly, winding a tight bud center.

2. Wind rose looser with more gathers toward outside of bud, and keep selvages in same plane on outer wraps. Roll about 5½ times, whipstitching edges as you go.

3. To finish rose (right), fold lips near center toward outside, pushing center up slightly; fold outer lips inward, if desired.

4. Tuck a fringed center of shaded ribbon into the center. Use ½-in.-wide moss-green satin ribbon for leaves. Cut a 3-in. piece for a center leaf and fold and tack complementary 60 degree angles toward the center. Repeat at each end of the 6-in. piece for two side leaves. Tack the leaves behind the rose.

Open rolled rose

Machine or hand gather along center of 24 in. of 1½-in.-wide yellow-to-fuschia shaded wire ribbon. Fold ribbon in half, and start rolling a tight bud center as above but with folded edge at base, wire edges up and yellow side inside. Roll firmly around core four times, stitching back and forth through bud's base to hold. Make next two rows slightly less gathered, but take tucks to add fullness that will allow petals to lie flat. Unfold last 6 in. of ribbon and pull inner wire to gather yellow edge tightly, as shown. Fold yellow side in toward center and continue winding rose and sewing yellow edge to core. To end off, roll fuschia edge up and under top of flower, and secure raw edge underneath.

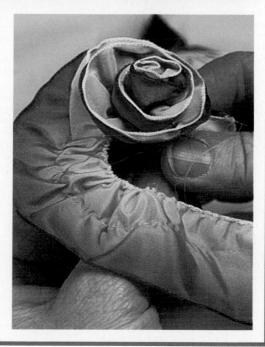

Ruching a ribbon camelia

Many ruching patterns make good flower petals. But this zigzag pattern is particularly successful for creating rounded petals. I used it on the primroses (at far left center of my block) as well as on the camelia. Use salmon-to-red 1-in.-wide shaded wire ribbon. Start with a yard and tailor to size as you build it.

Fold the ribbon as shown below to form the ruching pattern. Then ruche as shown below right. Bring the thread around the edge of the ribbon to the other side at the selvages—this nips the petals in perfectly. To avoid breaking the thread, stitch only six petals before gathering (each triangle is a petal).

Finally, fold the petals into a circle as shown in the photo below. The camelia will have four pink petals standing up in the center surrounded by as many concentric rounds of red petals as you desire. Finish it with a stamen made with a ¾-in. length of 1-in.-wide yellow ribbon. Fray ¼ in. at the top, roll the ribbon, and bind the bottom with thread or wire. Then tuck it into the center of the camelia. —E.S.

Ruching for petals

A light center and dark outer petals form a camelia.

1. Fold a zigzag sewing pattern into the ribbon: Hold raw end in left hand, and fold ribbon down at a right angle. Continue folding right angles for length of ribbon.

Fold line

2. Sew running stitch following first crease. At selvage, bring thread around edge and resume sewing along next crease.

Forming center:
1. Ruche so that there are six triangles on light side, five on dark side. Gather thread.
2. Curve petals around in circle over raw end with four light petals standing up in center.
3. Overlap fifth light petal with first dark petal, turning light petal in toward core of flower. Stitch corner of fifth dark petal under corner of first dark petal and pull ruched strip under flower to begin second row.

Outer petals:
Appliqué each outer petal of center to just cover gathering line of second row. In second and subsequent rows, only red petals will show. Place them between petals and well appliquéd down to previous row.

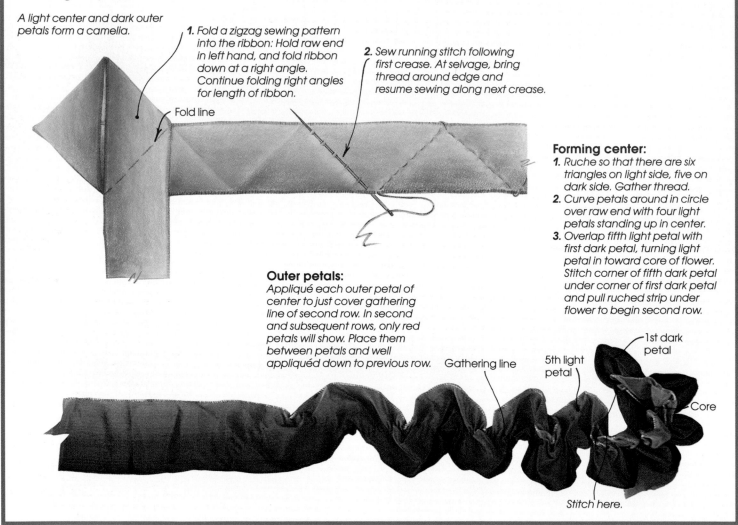

Gathering line

1st dark petal

5th light petal

Core

Stitch here.

Roses, the most frequently portrayed flower in the Baltimore album quilts and the heart of my block, symbolize love. As love, the rose is the essence of God's love for man, and the ideal of man's beneficence, one to another. A white rose means eternal love. A single rose expresses simplicity; a rose in full bloom says "I love you"; a musk rose stands for American beauty or means charming; a damask rose symbolizes a brilliant complexion or means the ambassador of love; and a China rose is for ever-fresh beauty. Rosebuds stand for beauty, purity, and youth; a moss rosebud says "I confess my love." A crown of roses, as in the "Crown of Ruched Roses" block that I'm finishing in the photo on p. 31, symbolizes superior merit, and a garland of roses means "virtue's reward."

Bluebells mean delicacy and constancy. And *lilies of the valley* say "Let us make up," and express sweetness, renewed happiness, spring, the birth of Christ, immortality, the tears of the Virgin Mary, and motherhood. *Primroses* (five-petaled posies) stand for early youth and young love. And a *red camelia* means unpretentious excellence. ☐

The sixth book in Elly Sienkiewicz's series on Baltimore album quilts, Dimensional Appliqué—Baskets, Blooms, and Baltimore Borders, was published by C&T Publishing in 1993 (5021 Blum St., Suite 1; Martinez, CA 94553-4307; 800-284-1114). Among other things, the book offers many more dimensional flowers.

Hawaiian Scrap Coverlet

Piecing directly to a backing eliminates quilting

by Lilo Markrich

Hawaiian Juana Talon has combined her Filipino traditions of frugality and scrap quilting in her own interpretation of traditional patchwork. The result is very precise self-lined squares strip-pieced from scraps of varying width. (Photo by Susan Kahn)

for nearly forty years, Juana Talon's daughters and granddaughters have been trying to learn how she makes her much-sought-after patchwork baby blankets and coverlets, shown above. But her explanation that it is all a matter of squares has always raised more questions than it answered. Since Juana is a woman of few words who loves any time-saving device, a suggestion that she sew in front of a video cam-

era made sense. From the videotape, I was able to see clearly how the square is at the heart of every project. And now we all know how Juana pieces and lines each square in one operation and how she backs and frames her unbatted coverlets with a second, related technique.

The values of a lifetime

Juana, who admits to 90, calls her blanket making "patching," a skill she takes for granted. After all, when she grew up, every rural Filipino woman taught her

daughters how to sew, embroider, and make blankets. But Juana Talon's "patching" is more than a treasured family gift. The way she incorporates fabric scraps with worn, discarded Aloha shirts, even one from a car rental agency (see the right-hand photo on p. 37), reveals her technique and uninhibited mix of patterns and fabrics as the living evidence of a once indigenous Hawaiian plantation folk art. Her work serves as a vivid reminder of a bygone way of life, where necessity never failed to challenge a woman's

Patching a square

Every block in Juana Talon's quilts consists of pieces of scrap fabric sewn to a square of lining.

Making a lining template

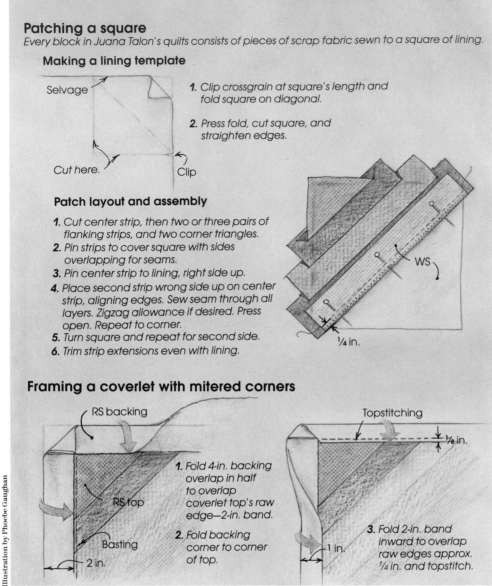

Selvage

1. Clip crossgrain at square's length and fold square on diagonal.

2. Press fold, cut square, and straighten edges.

Cut here.

Clip

Patch layout and assembly

1. Cut center strip, then two or three pairs of flanking strips, and two corner triangles.
2. Pin strips to cover square with sides overlapping for seams.
3. Pin center strip to lining, right side up.
4. Place second strip wrong side up on center strip, aligning edges. Sew seam through all layers. Zigzag allowance if desired. Press open. Repeat to corner.
5. Turn square and repeat for second side.
6. Trim strip extensions even with lining.

WS

¼ in.

Framing a coverlet with mitered corners

RS backing

Topstitching

⅛ in.

RS top

Basting

2 in.

1. Fold 4-in. backing overlap in half to overlap coverlet top's raw edge—2-in. band.

2. Fold backing corner to corner of top.

1 in.

3. Fold 2-in. band inward to overlap raw edges approx. ¼ in. and topstitch.

Illustration by Phoebe Gaughan

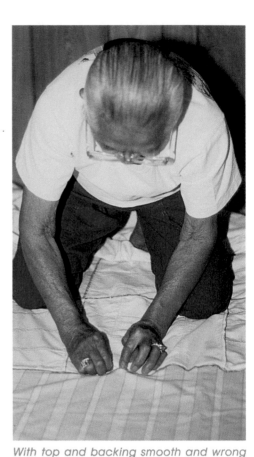

With top and backing smooth and wrong sides together, Juana folds the top back to expose the first strip-length seam allowance. She pins, then bastes it to the backing before machine sewing it. Any color thread is acceptable since no stitching shows on the front. She zigzags each seam allowance to the lining and overcasts each seam between squares and strips. (Photo by Kathleen Rakuya Markrich)

imagination and creative instincts.

Juana left Ilocos Norte in the Philippines for Hawaii in around 1920 after her young husband, who had found work on a sugar cane plantation on Maui, had saved enough money to send for her. Life on a plantation for women like Juana meant company housing, little cash, homesickness, rare contact with the outside world, and an unshakable determination to hold on to traditional cultural and spiritual values. The only resources a woman had were the skills her mother had taught her and her Catholic faith. Sewing the family's clothing and household furnishings was as much part of her everyday life as raising children, cooking, cleaning, growing vegetables, and practicing the utmost frugality.

Every scrap of fabric, including rice bags and burlap sacking, was saved and used. A pieced pair of cotton trunks was as common as a pieced lining. A plantation worker's wife bought yardage only when the occasion demanded, such as a child's baptism or first communion, and every fabric or clothing purchase was seen as a future contribution to the family's scrap bag. As soon as there were enough scraps, work began on another coverlet.

Juana spent her evenings making squares. When she had enough, she joined and lined them, and another coverlet was ready for use. But it never occurred to her that anything made out of scraps had any value other than practical or that "patching" could be used for gifts.

Sometime around 1950, widowed, fiercely independent, and saddened that she had little to give as family gifts, Juana took the advice of her sister and an old girlfriend that she use her bags of scraps to make fancy gift quilts. Seeing traditional patchwork quilts, she realized that instead of cutting scraps into squares, which were then joined to make rice-bag-lined cotton blankets, other women made squares with many small scraps. For Juana, this concept had several advantages. It was an even more economical use of scraps, and if she made her new squares pretty enough, she wouldn't be embarrassed to give them as gifts. Organizing her scraps into multicolored squares became her all-consuming passion.

Planning a coverlet

Family and friends have kept Juana well supplied with old clothes and scraps. She doesn't mind if one of her daughters buys a colorful remnant she can use as a backing, but she still considers it a terrible waste to cut a sizable remnant or new fabric into small pieces. How the coverlet is going to evolve depends on how many bits and pieces she *thinks* she can cut out of this or that shirt, pair of shorts, or sewing waste and on how big a coverlet she wants to make. If it is for a new baby, it will be small, maybe 24 by 36 in. That may mean that she has to make twenty-four 6-in. squares. If she thinks she can find enough pieces to make a large coverlet (the one on p. 35 is 70 in. square) her squares might be as large as 12 in.

Once she has decided on the overall size and the number of squares, Juana starts looking for pieces that will look nice together. Color influences her more than pattern. She has no problem mixing sailboats with flowering hibiscus, promotional themes (right-hand photo below), and provincial prints. The next step is to see how many small scraps she can cut into triangles, squares, or strips and how many she needs to join for a square. One of her unwritten rules is never to cut up a large piece of fabric if a small piece will do.

Making a square

All coverlets are made by covering a lining square with colorful patches, joining squares into strips, strips into a top, and then lining and edging the top. From Juana's point of view, knowing how to cut cloth to avoid any waste has always been more important than the sewing. She gauges the amount of cloth for a gusset with her forefinger and thumb; she gauges length and width with the edge of her hand, the distance from the tip of her small finger to her wrist joint. Nothing has convinced her that any other way of measuring cloth is superior.

Before Juana begins to assemble her scraps for squares, she cuts a lining square of unbleached muslin. The way she makes that first square, which becomes the template for all the other lining squares (see the top drawing on the facing page), is a good example of how she measures and cuts. She double-checks that all edges are straight and even by folding the square diagonally, horizontally, and vertically, and she trims it as necessary.

The colored patches—With the template square ironed and on the floor, Juana now chooses fabric strips that will cover it. For the pattern (center drawing on the facing page), she begins with a strip that covers the square's center diagonally. If it is too long, she folds it back on itself at one corner of the square and trims it. She trues each strip as she cuts it by folding it in half lengthwise and trimming its edges. Then she pins it to the lining square.

The colors of the central strip determine what she will use next, and she cuts pairs of strips to go on either side of the center. She gauges their length and width by aligning them against the preceding strip and overlapping to allow for seams. Finally she fills the square by adding triangular corner pieces.

Assembly—Sewing and lining is one operation, as shown in the center drawing. But before sewing, Juana irons the lining and patches. Every time she sews a seam,

no matter how small, Juana stops to press, which she considers the most important step. First she presses as sewn with the top strip wrong side up. Then she turns the top strip face up and presses from the top. Often, she'll stitch or zigzag each seam again over the allowance to give the square extra body.

When she has made as many squares as she thinks she'll need, she's ready to arrange them. She especially enjoys this process because no two squares are ever alike. If she thinks that the blanket ought to be bigger or something seems to be missing, she makes more squares, even if she can't match the fabrics. She then joins groups of squares into lengthwise strips, basting or pinning before seaming. To prevent the seam from fraying and to add body, she overcasts or zigzags the edge. Overcast seams are pressed in the same direction. Then she joins the strips, perhaps turning them in opposite directions to make a new pattern.

Backing the coverlet

Juana's choice for the backing, a large piece of material, seems to depend as much on cost as suitability. The fabric must be sturdy and 4 in. larger on all sides than the top. She secures the backing to her top of joined strips by placing the top "back to back" (wrong side to wrong side) on the backing 4 in. from the backing's edge. She pins the edge of the coverlet top that runs parallel to the strips to the backing, then bastes and sews it. She returns the two layers to the floor and turns the top back until she finds the seam between the first two strips. Now she smooths the lining and bastes the strip's seam allowance to it, pinning first to hold it, as shown in the photo on the facing page. She then stitch-

es the seam allowance to the lining with a straight or zigzag stitch (often both) and leaves the basting as well. She presses it three ways— as sewn, opened from the top, and from the back. Then she returns to the floor and repeats the process for the next strip.

With the backing firmly attached to the top, she's ready for the final step, framing her coverlet with the 4 in. of backing that still extends on all sides. One side at a time, she folds the band in half toward the center, bastes, and presses. Then she turns in each corner to miter it, as shown in the bottom drawings on the facing page. Topstitching along the inner, folded edge of the frame is often two lines of straight stitch and a colorful zigzag trim.

Juana's coverlets are never for sale, and in a world where the appliquéd, echo-quilted Hawaiian quilt dominates all other Hawaiian ethnic folk arts and crafts, an old-fashioned plantation skill attracts little attention. But in looking at and using Juana's quilts, one can sense the pleasure she has always found in meeting the challenges of her life. Perhaps that is the secret of her youthful and adventurous spirit. Looking at the coverlets she describes as "something new," as shown below, you know that she has seen an advertisement for a traditional quilt or pattern and has decided to make one just like it, unaware that her interpretation is always very different. □

Lilo Markrich is a contributing editor of Threads. *Juana is her granddaughter Mikayla's great-grandmother. Lilo would like to thank Mikayla's other grandmother, Philomena Rakuya, for her insights on plantation life and Michael and Kathleen Markrich for capturing Juana Talon's creative spirit on film.*

Juana applies her strip-piecing technique to more complex patterns like a pinwheel (left) and star (right). First she pieces small shapes together to form strips, then she sews the strips to the lining. (Photos by Sandra Markrich)

Tahitian Papercut Quilts

Cutting a design from one piece of folded fabric creates the appliqué for a *tifaifai*

by Roxanne McElroy

ahiti. The name alone conjures up exotic images and romantic thoughts. It is not surprising that, having been introduced to traditional quilting by Western missionaries, the creative and independent Tahitian women quickly developed their own exotic method of quilting. *Tifaifai* (I pronounce it *TEE fay fay*, which is easy for Westerners to say and fairly close to the true pronunciation) is the Tahitian word for sewing and has come to denote the two-layer, unbatted, appliqué quilts the Tahitian women make.

I believe that the creative Tahitian women adapted their design method from a simple folded papercutting technique introduced by some of the island's visitors. The sewing method they developed looks difficult but is really the simplest type of freeform appliqué. Because the *tifaifai* is one continuous layer of fabric appliquéd to another of a strongly contrasting color, there are no rough seam allowances on the back, so it was easy to eliminate the quilting process altogether. Tahitians just hem all the edges of the quilt top and use it as a lightweight spread, which certainly makes sense in a tropical jungle where no one ever needs a warm quilt. Their fabric is a medium-weight cotton that's a little heavier than American quilt fabrics.

There are only two rules in making a Tahitian quilt. First, the appliqué fabric must be folded into quarters so the de-sign can be cut out through the four layers at once. Then it is unfolded onto the base fabric for sewing. Second, in designing a *tifaifai*, the quilt maker must make the subject of the quilt something that has influenced her in her daily life. It is only when a Tahitian decides to honor a specific item or event that a design is made, and no Tahitian exactly copies another's design. I find this second rule a very exciting concept because every quilt maker has been influenced by specific events or things, and Tahitian quilting gives us the opportunity to honor those things in a special and personal way. It's also a lot of fun to design your own four-fold appliqué pattern.

Drawing the design

Most Tahitian women draw only one-quarter of their symmetrical appliqué de-sign and visualize what it will look like when the four-fold fabric is opened out onto the base fabric. Making a design this way is like cutting paper dolls or snowflakes. If you find visualizing too difficult, you can certainly draw the entire design in miniature and then make your quarter-size pattern for cutting from one quadrant. A quarter drawing of about 40 by 42 in. will fit nicely on a double-size quilt, 84 by 96 in., with a 2-in. border and hem allowance.

If you desire a single item in the center of your quilt—a wreath, medallion, etc. (see the photo on p. 42)—it must be sym-metrical with only one quadrant drawn. Remember, every item you draw will actually show up on the quilt four times, as you can see in the photo on the facing page. So you must pay particular attention to the fold edges of the design, which fall at the fabric axes. It is nice to make two leaves come together at the fold; or if you're using a symmetrical flower or plant, as I did on the quilt on the facing page, you can place half of it along the fold so that when it is cut and unfolded it will be whole. Be sure to incorporate connectors of some sort into the design at the fold so the four quarters don't fall apart when you unfold the cutout.

Designs with detached borders, like the "Hibiscus" quilt being made in the photos on p. 40, are also traditional. When Tahi-tians do this, they always cut "bridges" in strategic places to hold the border to the main part of the design until it has been laid out and pinned. Bridges can also be used between items within the central portion of the design if there is a lot of open area between them. This makes it easier to align the appliqué when you're

Traditional Tahitian quilts have a four-way, symmetrical design that stands out boldly because of the strongly contrasted solid colors. Roxanne McElroy added a lot of detail to her unusual "Mermaids" quilt with channel appliqué, one of her favorite techniques. (Photo by Susan Kahn)

From *Threads* magazine (September 1992) 42:36-41

Hold your scissor blades exactly perpendicular to the fabric as you cut so all four layers will be identical. "Bridges," indicated by dotted lines, keep the separate border attached to the field temporarily.

After the entire appliqué piece has been cut out, use a small rotary cutter and mat to cut open all the detail lines. When you sew them with channel appliqué, they will form ¼-in.-wide slits that add a dimension of realism to the design.

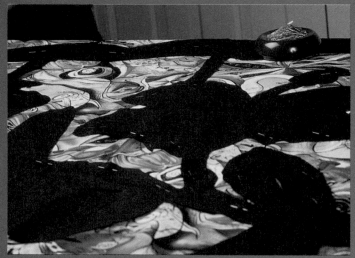

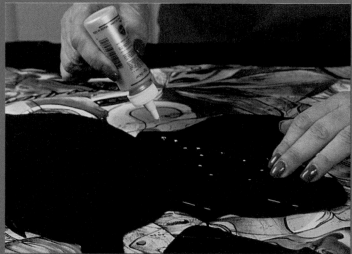

The tifaifai is laid out and pinned one quarter at a time. The bridge near the pin container was accidentally severed during cutting, so the quilters marked it lightly with pencil so they could line it up at this crucial point.

Aleene's School Glue, which is entirely water soluble, is ideal for speed basting. Place small dots every inch, ½ in. from all raw edges, and pat the appliqué lightly. The severed bridge, now no longer necessary, has just been removed.

laying it out. If you make a mistake and accidently cut through a bridge, just use a pencil to mark the place where the bridge should connect so you'll be able to abut it when laying out the piece.

Preparing the fabric

Tahitian quilts were traditionally made with two solid-colored, highly contrasting fabrics. Now that prints are more readily available, Tahitian women are using them as well. You must prewash and iron your fabric because if the two large pieces that you are appliquéing together shrink at different rates, which is likely, distortion will be severe. It would be terrible to have all your careful sewing ruined by the first wash.

All *tifaifai* are made by folding two quilt-sized pieces of fabric in quarters—first in half lengthwise, then crosswise. *Press very crisp fold lines* into both pieces

before beginning the project because you'll need them to align the appliqué.

Tahitians often sew two pieces of fabric together to acquire the width needed to make a quilt. The least noticeable place to put the seam is right down the middle. To make a quilt with a finished size of 84 by 108 in., I buy six yards of 44- or 45-in.-wide cotton fabric for both the appliqué piece and the background. I cut each into two 3-yard pieces, and join each pair of pieces along the straight grain.

If you plan to quilt your *tifaifai*, sew the two lengths of fabric for each layer together with a ¼-in. seam allowance, and press both allowances to one side for added strength. If you do not plan to quilt, use a flat-fell seam (see *Basics, Threads*, No. 42, p. 18) down the middle of the background fabric to finish it. I also recommend that this piece be a little heavier than the appliqué piece if you're not go-

ing to quilt. Sew the appliqué fabric with a plain ¼-in. seam pressed to one side.

It is also exciting to design and plan Tahitian quilts on a smaller scale for wall hangings. I make my quarter drawing approximately 20 by 22 in. so I can take advantage of the full width of standard quilters' cotton fabrics and make my finished wall hanging 44 by 48 in.

Cutting out the appliqué

Before you begin cutting out your appliqué, it is a good idea to shade or darken the actual design on the paper pattern so you won't become confused once the cutting is underway.

It is easiest simply to pin the paper pattern to the folded fabric and cut it out as you would a dress pattern. Most paper of large size is heavy, however, so I recommend that you use long, strong quilting pins rather than fine silk pins. Pin the pattern to the folded cloth, aligning the center at the corner where the folds meet and placing the edges right on the folds.

Most Tahitian women don't have access to large pieces of paper, so they tape shopping bags together to draw a pattern. They lay sheets of pencil carbon paper over the appliqué fabric (which is folded wrong side out), place the paper pattern on top, and trace the design onto the fabric with a ballpoint pen. This way they can reuse a design or the paper it's drawn on. They then cut just outside the carbon lines through all four layers.

You'll need a very sharp pair of scissors to cut through all the layers at once without disturbing them. Be as careful as you can to keep the scissors perfectly perpendicular to the fabric so that the four layers are cut identically, as shown at top left, facing page. Precision in cutting, however, is only as important as you think it is. If you make a little miscut, don't panic. You can usually hide the error in the appliqué process, or you can make it look intentional. Besides, since a miscut will show up four times, the symmetry will be unaffected.

A *tifaifai* seam allowance is never more than ⅛ in., so I don't allow for it when drawing or cutting out a design. Details in the design, like flower petals and leaf veins at right or mermaid scales on p. 39, are frequently done with channel appliqué. I indicate them on my patterns as a simple line. When you cut out the pattern, cut these lines open too. I use my small rotary cutter and mat, as shown at top right, facing page. In sewing, these raw edges will be appliquéd with ⅛-in. seam allowances, leaving a ¼-in.-wide channel.

Laying out the *tifaifai*

It's helpful to have a large, flat surface on which to work, such as a Ping-Pong table. You can reduce back strain by placing paint cans, blocks, or bricks under the table's legs to raise it to a more comfortable height. Unfold the background fabric and lay it on the table right side up. The point where the fold lines intersect is the center of the quilt. Place it on the center of the table. Carefully unfold the cut-out appliqué piece. First, find its center and pin it, right side up, over the exact center of the

background piece with the folds of both pieces intersecting.

Laying out the appliqué piece is not difficult if you first match fold lines out to the edges and pin them in place so they can't shift. Now you can shift the entire project so that one quarter at a time is on the table to be pinned. Pay close attention to the grain of the two fabrics to help you decide the angle of an extending flower or leaf. Tahitian women spend an enjoyable amount of time just lightly patting the fabric into its proper place with their hands, rather than lifting and replacing it over and over again. They call this process "pat-pat," and it's probably a throwback to the ancient, rhythmic pounding of tapa cloth.

Refer to the original drawing or picture to find out how close or how far things should be from each other. Pin the first quarter (except bridges) temporarily, as shown at lower left, facing page, and move the entire project to another quarter. When all four quarters have been pinned, use a yardstick to be sure that the borders are all the same distance from the

An afternoon quilting bee (facing page) prepared "Hibiscus" so McElroy could complete the quilting on her own. Prints are becoming increasingly popular in Tahiti, but if you decide to use them, you must be careful to maintain a strong contrast between fabrics. (Photo by Susan Kahn)

edge of the background fabric and that they're all perfectly straight. Now you can cut off the bridges—unless you are not going to baste the quilt right away.

You must baste the entire *tifaifai* ½ in. from *all* raw edges to keep it from shifting as you appliqué. Pin basting is impossible on a project of this size because you must gather the entire thing up in your hand to work in the center, and the pins (or safety pins) will cause you continual agony. Basting a *tifaifai* usually takes the better part of a day. Or you can use a product that has certainly made my life easier: Aleene's School Glue (available in most general crafts stores).

I put little dots of the water-soluble glue ½ in. from raw edges about 1 in. apart to baste the layers together, as shown in the lower right-hand photo on the facing page. I'm careful not to press down on the glued places until they are dry, to ensure that the glue isn't actually pressed into the fibers of the fabric. This glue will come out completely in the first wash. Be sure to wash the quilt top before sandwiching it for quilting (if desired) so you won't have to quilt through hard spots of glue.

Sewing the *tifaifai*

A *tifaifai* is the perfect appliqué quilt to practice with because it is the most forgiving of error. If your points aren't perfectly sharp, it's all right because they will at least be consistent throughout the quilt; their shape will look "planned."

Having sewn many *tifaifai* in the last few years, I've developed some special techniques to make needle-turn appliqué less intimidating. I've explained them on the next two pages. (Also, take a look at "Alphabet Appliqué" in *Quilts and Quilting*, Taunton Press, 1991; p. 73.)

The one thing to remember about making a *tifaifai* is that it should be fun. *Maita'i manuia*—Good luck!

Roxanne McElroy lived in Tahiti for three years, which gave her the chance to learn tifaifai *making from the experts. She sells her own Tahitian-style patterns; for information, contact Designs by Roxanne, 8485 Sentinae Chase Dr., Roswell, GA 30076; (404) 640-6711.* ⇨

Needle-turn appliqué

Needle-turn appliqué takes its name from the fact that you use the point or the shank of the needle, as appropriate, to turn under the seam allowance as you sew. You never use pressing, templates, freezer paper, etc., so the technique is also sometimes called freeform appliqué. You can use whatever size needle you prefer; I generally use a long, thin needle, usually a size 10 sharp.

Always work from right to left if you are right-handed (left to right if you are left-handed). With the eye of your needle at about 2 o'clock (10 o'clock if you're left-handed) and the basted *tifaifai* on your lap with the raw edge you're about to sew parallel to your body, practice "scrubbing" the raw

"Ferns" is a traditional Tahitian tifaifai *pattern. The detached border on this design makes it a bit tricky to cut and lay out precisely. Fern details are achieved with channel appliqué and many outside and inside points and inside curves. (Photo by Susan Kahn)*

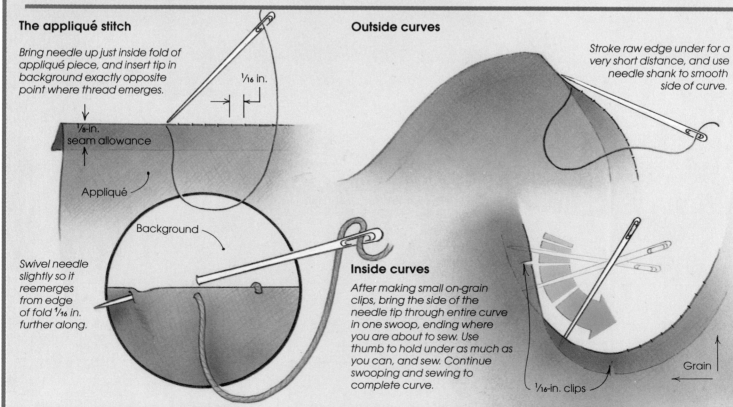

The appliqué stitch

Bring needle up just inside fold of appliqué piece, and insert tip in background exactly opposite point where thread emerges.

1/16 in.

1/8-in. seam allowance

Appliqué

Background

Swivel needle slightly so it reemerges from edge of fold 1/16 in. further along.

Outside curves

Stroke raw edge under for a very short distance, and use needle shank to smooth side of curve.

Inside curves

After making small on-grain clips, bring the side of the needle tip through entire curve in one swoop, ending where you are about to sew. Use thumb to hold under as much as you can, and sew. Continue swooping and sewing to complete curve.

1/16-in. clips

Grain

edge of the fabric down toward you with the needle tip and sliding your left thumb up over the fold thus made to keep it in place. The goal is to tuck ⅛ in. of raw edge under and hold it down with your thumb. Normally, it is possible to fold under and finger press about 1½ in. ahead of where you are working.

The stitch—Hide the knot under the folded edge, and stitch through the fold about two threads in from the edge, bringing the needle up on the outside. Insert the needle exactly beside where the thread is coming out of the folded edge, but just off the edge through the base fabric. Change the needle's angle and come up about ¹⁄₁₆ in. away from the first stitch two threads inside the folded edge, as shown in the drawings at left, facing page. Pull the thread tight enough to bury itself in the fiber of the fabric but not so tight that the fabric puckers.

Tight outside curves—Depending on the tightness of the curve, you can turn under only very small amounts ahead of your work—sometimes only enough for two or three stitches at a time. Use the needle point to pull out areas that may have been tucked under too far, and use the side of the needle to help mold a perfectly smooth curved edge, as shown in the top right drawing,

facing page. Finger pressing is very helpful to keep the fold exactly where you want it.

Tight inside curves—Take advantage of the fact that all fabrics stretch on the bias, and make allowances for the fact that no fabrics give with the grain by making a ¹⁄₁₆-in. clip on the north, south, east, and west of the curve on the grain (most curves will include only one or two of these on-grain compass points). Reach as far as your hand will swivel to the counterclockwise edge of the curve. Start applying pressure with the side of the needle to turn under the entire curve back to where you are to sew in one swoop, as shown in the lower right drawing, facing page.

You can't hold the entire tuck under with your thumb, but hold as much as you can while you take a few stitches. Repeat the process as you go until you have stitched down the entire curve. You'll find that it turns under very easily with no more than four clips.

Outside points—Appliqué to within an inch of the point. Then needle-turn the raw edge under *all the way through the point*. You can cut off the little wing that sticks out underneath the raw edge as well as a bit of that edge. Continue to appliqué until you come close enough to the point to be within the imagined seam allowance of the edge on the other

side of the point, as shown in the drawing at upper left, below. Turn your work clockwise to make it easier to cram the raw point down and under in a sort of counterclockwise motion *as far as you can*, and hold it down lightly with your thumb. Don't worry that you crammed too much under because if you tug at the end of your thread, the point will pop out to exactly where you wanted it to be. Take one very small stitch to secure the point, as shown in the drawing at lower left. If you can, reach under with a pair of embroidery scissors and trim some of the seam allowance to eliminate the bulk. Needle-turn appliqué down the other side.

Sharp inside points—You must plan ahead for inside points. Appliqué only until you are about 1 in. from the inside point and stop. With the needle, turn the seam allowance under, gently tapering it to nothing at the point, as shown below. Hold it down with your thumb and appliqué. Make your stitches increasingly closer as you approach the point because so little is turned under. Take two or three tiny stitches in the point itself to reinforce it. Now, starting about 1 in. up the other side with a normal seam allowance, gently taper back down to nothing at the point. Appliqué with very small stitches, gradually increasing to normal size for the first inch. —*R.M.*

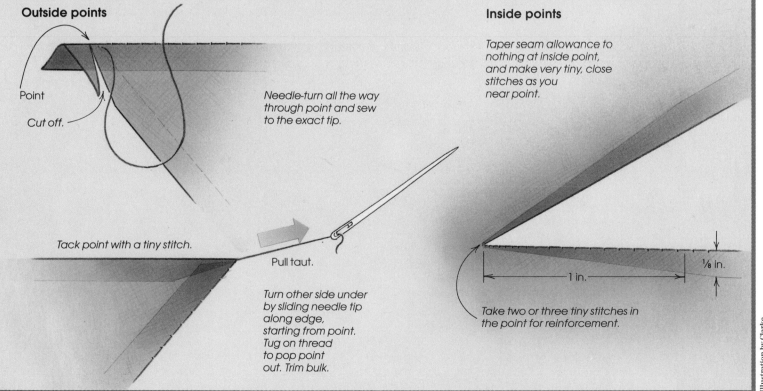

Outside points

Point

Cut off.

Tack point with a tiny stitch.

Needle-turn all the way through point and sew to the exact tip.

Pull taut.

Turn other side under by sliding needle tip along edge, starting from point. Tug on thread to pop point out. Trim bulk.

Inside points

Taper seam allowance to nothing at inside point, and make very tiny, close stitches as you near point.

1 in.

⅛ in.

Take two or three tiny stitches in the point for reinforcement.

Illustration by Clarke

No-Template Piecing

Rotary-cut strips make triangles and
small pieces easy to handle

by Elizabeth Hoffman and Shannon Rettig

From *Threads* magazine (July 1993) 47:54-57

*i*f you've ever tried to sew together extremely small pieces of fabric, you know that the process can quickly become a nightmare. Pieces shift, seamlines waver, and corners refuse to meet. We've developed an approach that helps prevent these problems and can significantly improve the accuracy and efficiency of your cutting and piecing.

All these benefits come from two related ideas. The first is that we almost never stitch triangular pieces by cutting out the triangle and stitching along its stretchy bias edges. Instead, we cut a square or rectangle and stitch along the diagonal to form the triangle, trimming off the unused portion along the seamline. Because the rest of the square is still there when we're stitching, the bias seamline remains stable—at the cost of some fabric waste. We've decided the results are worth it.

Of course this idea only works with right triangles, which can be trimmed from squares or rectangles, but this leads to the second idea. We plan our quilt blocks and motifs so that all or most of the pieces we need to cut are squares and rectangles. Before you decide that this would be too limiting, take a look at the basket block in the photo on the facing page. Although this 4-in. block looks as if it were made almost entirely from triangles, we worked only with squares and rectangles. The process is shown step by step in the photos at right. When we want curves (like the basket handles) or other pieces that we can't get from rectangles, we appliqué them.

The block on the facing page may look like it's all triangles, but except for the appliquéd bias handles, it's stitched entirely from squares and rectangles. To learn how it was done, read on.

Cutting squares and rectangles means not only that almost all our pieces are cut on grain, which reduces stretching when the pieces are handled and sewn, but it also makes accurate cutting a snap. We've taken this idea to its logical conclusion by choosing to lay out all our designs to fit precisely on the lines of graph paper. This way we can do away with patterns and templates altogether, cutting quickly and accurately with a rotary cutter and a clearly marked, transparent quilters' ruler. On the following pages you'll find a step-by-step description of how to plan and complete a complex block in this way.

These techniques, combined with the construction tips that follow, have freed us to undertake pieced pictorial quilts

Right triangles from squares

Triangles are difficult to sew accurately because the bias edges stretch. But if you sew a square along the diagonal, you get the desired triangle easily because you're using much more stable pieces. In this traditional-looking basket block, all pieces are cut as either squares or rectangles except the bias-cut handles, which are appliquéd to the center square first. Draw your block and measure finished dimensions. Cut all pieces allowing ¼-in. seam allowances on all sides (i.e., ½ in. wider and longer than desired finished size).

1 *Cut center square.*

2 *Cut basket squares. (Side of basket is ½ finished side of center square plus seam allowances.) Align seam allowances of each basket with center square at corner, and sew right sides together. (Draw diagonal with pencil on wrong side.) Press right sides up, and trim seam allowance to ¼ in. by cutting away underportion of basket square.*

3 *Cut rectangles in background fabric for block sides (length equals length of block minus twice the rectangle's width, plus allowances). Cut two squares' width of rectangle for base of each basket. With right sides together, sew basket-base squares to each end of rectangle. Press open. Then sew to sides of center.*

4 *Cut background squares for corners. Align corners at base of basket, right sides together, and sew as in step 2. Press open and trim excess underneath.*

made from hundreds of tiny pieces, like the one in the small detail photo on p. 46, without going crazy.

Measuring and cutting

Before you begin cutting small pieces, it's a good idea to cut the quilt's borders. This way you'll know you have enough length.

Since your pattern is in finished dimensions, you must add ¼-in. seam allowances to all sides of each pattern piece. For example, if a pattern piece measures 2 by 4 in., use your rotary cutter and acrylic ruler to cut a rectangle 2½ by

4½ in. All edges of squares and rectangles should be cut on straight grain to help prevent stretching. We only deviate from this rule when a bias cut will enhance the design. Plaids and stripes in particular invite interesting design possibilities when cut out on bias.

Mirror-image pattern pieces can be cut by placing multiple layers of fabric with right sides together. Also, cut as many pieces as you can from one fabric at a time, rather than cutting some from one piece of fabric, some from another, and then going back to the first piece again. As

Assembling complex shapes and designs from rotary-cut strips lets you piece a picture rather than appliqué it. Almost every element of "Charmed Woods" (detail), designed and sewn by Shannon Rettig, is built of rectangles and squares, plus a few triangles.

you cut and sew, place pieces on a wall (cotton batt holds them securely) so you can see from a distance how the colors and shapes are working.

Sewing

We use a shorter machine-stitch length than usual for our techniques, approximately 13 sts/in. (a ¼-in. piece is held together by three stitches.) Stitching an accurate ¼-in. seam allowance is critical. If your presser foot is not ¼ in. wide, mark the front of your throat plate with tape.

Don't backstitch. Seams will be secured when another line of stitching crosses them. Backstitching causes bulk, may cause fabric bunching in small pieces, and is more difficult to rip out. If you rip and distortion occurs, cut a new piece.

Chain sew whenever possible: sew all pieces for a section of the block in order without cutting the thread between them or raising the presser foot. Because the fabric will feed evenly, there will be less distortion. It will also save time and thread and keep pieces in sequence. To prevent the first piece from bunching, run a test piece through at the start of the chain.

Pin critical intersections, but use as few pins as possible, and don't sew over them. Use shorter sequin pins, poke through the fabric to match points, and let pins dangle. Matching pieces with different shapes (as in the the house block on the facing page) can be difficult. One solution is to fold each piece in half, slightly marking the midpoint with a crease.

Pressing

After accurate cutting, pressing is most critical for crisp points and corners. Finger pressing is a good start to open the seams. You need a good iron with a cotton setting and steam action, that's comfortable and dependable. *Pressing* involves

the lifting and pressing down of the iron, not moving it sideways (*ironing*), which can cause distortion. Circumstances dictate the best pressing direction:

• Sewing across seams that have been pressed in alternate directions helps control *bulk*. Sewing across seams pressed in the same direction can cause slippage.

• For mirror-image pieces, pressing should be *symmetrical*. Otherwise the added bulk of the seam will lift a design area on one side and not the other.

• Press seams *away from a point*.

• Think of potential quilting. Areas that are raised due to added layers of seam allowances underneath create *depth*. You can achieve greater depth in these raised areas by quilting in the ditch.

• If the underlying seam allowances *show through* lighter fabrics, press toward darker values. Allowances may not be as obvious with batt and backing attached. □

Shannon Rettig and Elizabeth Hoffman are quiltmakers and teachers who share a passion for the history and the process of making quilts. A pattern for "Charmed Woods" (detail above) is available from Quiltwork Patches (see "Further Reading").

Further reading

All books are available by mail from Quiltwork Patches, 209 S.W. 2nd St., PO Box 724, Corvallis, OR 97339; (503) 752-4820.

Hughes, T. **Template-Free Quiltmaking.** Bothell, WA: That Patchwork Place, 1986.

McCloskey, M. **Guide to Rotary Cutting.** Seattle, WA: Feathered Star Productions, 1990.

Thomas, D.L. **Shortcuts: A Concise Guide to Rotary Cutting.** Bothell, WA: That Patchwork Place, 1991.

Planning and piecing a template-free pattern

Template-free cutting depends on both your pattern and your cutting guide—a transparent ruler, used with a rotary cutter—being based on the same grid. Most quilters' rulers are marked with ¼-in. lines or grids, so to work with these, plan (or adjust) your design to fit on the lines of ¼-in. graph paper, like the house block on the facing page. Some rulers have ⅛-in. increments so you could use these with ⅛-in. paper for intricate designs. Either way, all your rectangular pieces can be cut using only the ruler's markings; you won't need a template. Simply add ½ in. (2 x ¼ in.) to the length and width for seam allowances.

Angles other than 45 degrees can be drawn, but the diagonals won't hit the corners of the stitching line. Consider appliquéing these shapes, along with curves and tiny pieces like the chimney in the design on the facing page. Delete lines that add unnecessary complications.

Once your design is drawn, the gridlines will make it easy to break it down into rectangular sections, which can each be completed separately before being assembled into the final block. The photos below show the process applied to the house design on the facing page.

Assembling the units

3 Assemble unit A as described on p. 45.

Place unit on top of pattern. If it isn't exactly finished size plus ¼ in. all the way around, try again.

4 Assemble unit B like unit A.

Reducing a grid-based block to rectangular units

All dimensions shown include ¼-in. seam allowances.

1 To sew a complex block efficiently, first identify the elements that can be grouped together into rectangles. Remember: each line is a seamline.

In this case, units A and B are identical rectangular strips with triangular elements added.

Units C and D are squares assembled from vertical strips

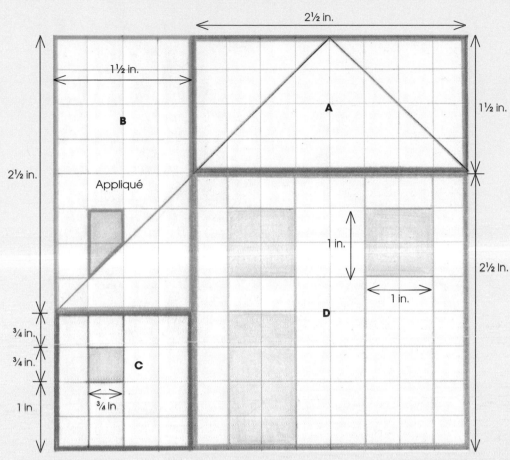

2 Measure the pattern. Add ¼-in. seam allowances on all sides of all pieces (plus ½ in. in length and width). Write these cutting measurements on pattern, if desired. Then cut strips of fabric in widths needed for each color.

All pieces for units A and B are cut from 1½-in.-wide strips, which include ¼-in. seam allowances.

Units C and D are cut from ¾-in.-wide and 1-in.-wide strips, including seam allowances.

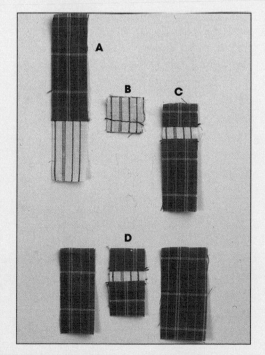

5 Unit C is composed of three strips, with a ¼-in. window in the center strip. When working with such small pieces, it's easier to sew longer strips together, then trim to size.

A. Sew two strips together for ¾-in. pieces.

B. Trim to desired size for window and piece above it (remember seam allowances).

C. Use trimmed-off piece for strip under window, and trim to unit size.

D. Attach side strips to window unit, and trim off irregular lengths to unit size.

6 Unit D is assembled like unit C.

7 With all units completed, you're ready to join them into a block, sewing only straight seams. Join A to D, then B to C, and finally AD to BC. Then add any appliqués.

Necktie Legacy

A father's collection lives on in pieced and pleated garment details

by Nancy O. Bryant

the phone rang late on a Thursday night in July, 1986, while I was sewing. It was my mother calling. Dad had had a heart attack while on a bike ride with my older brother. He had died instantly.

Dad and I were very close, and good friends. Losing him was hard, even though I had activities to distract me.

About six months passed. While looking at magazine photographs one night, I was intrigued by an outfit made from men's neckties. My mind raced. Dad had loved clothes. And he had some great ties. I called Mom. No, she had not given away his ties, and yes, she would send them to me. Soon more than 30 ties arrived. I quickly arranged them into color groups with about four ties in each group.

Dad's ties seemed perfect for embellishing garments. My own designs often have been inspired by historic costume. But whereas each design had always had a unique focus, I now felt ready to approach garment design from a different perspective; I was ready to begin a series—the tie series—with each outfit using one of the color groups.

The author paid tribute to her late father by using his neckties in a series of garments. For "Egyptian Goddess" (shown at left), pleating turns a too-bold tie print into flickers of gold, white, and black for the back-center yoke. Pleated strips of black and gold tie fabrics border the yoke. (Photo by Susan Kahn)

From *Threads* magazine (September 1992) 42:54-57

The challenge of ties

You can most conveniently use ties when they're single thickness. Take apart the tie, remove the linings and interfacings, and press them flat. Dad's ties were made from gorgeous fabrics, so I wanted them to be as visible as possible. I also knew that I wanted the tie pieces to be part of the structure of the garment and an integral part of the design, not just details on a collar or cuffs. I wanted to use the tie pieces in long and narrow shapes, so that they would still be recognizable as having been neckties.

Ties typically have two piecing seams, one near the center back and another along the narrow end of the tie, yielding three sections of tie fabric (see photo below). The front section of the tie, when laid open, can be surprisingly wide. There is a small section where the tie wraps around the back of the neck. This piece is so narrow that in most cases it is useless for embellishing garments. The remaining section of the tie, which hangs underneath the front section when the tie is worn, is usually fairly long and narrow.

Working with necktie fabric is a real design challenge. The silk fabrics are slippery and delicate. Ties are traditionally cut on the bias to help the necktie conform to the curved neck shape and to form a flexible knot at the neck. However, when used in a garment, bias-cut pieces have a tendency to stretch, twist, and distort. I had to find ways to stabilize the bias-cut fabrics. At times, the bias cut can be an advantage. For example, a bias-cut collar made from a necktie will shape nicely around the neck.

Sometimes ties are cut on the partial bias, rather than the true bias, particularly the two smaller sections. (For a more detailed description of bias, see *Basics, Threads,* No. 42, p. 18). This was a problem especially for striped ties, because I usually wanted the stripes to meet and line up vertically, horizontally, or diagonally on the garment. I had to waste some fabric in recutting the tie section so that the stripes were aligned on the true bias.

To overcome the potential distortion problems of the bias-cut tie pieces, I decided to apply the pieces to a base garment fabric, rather than inlay them in a section of the garment. The stable base fabric would lessen the potential stretching and distortion of the bias tie pieces. Since there would be at least two thicknesses of fabric wherever the tie pieces were applied, these areas would be somewhat stiff, making fluid, draped styles not feasible.

Straight, stabilized piecing

I cut my teeth on "Turkoman Ties," shown in the left-hand photo on p. 51, the least difficult of the pieces I have completed thus far. This garment has a simple tubular shape that is not adversely affected by the stiffness from the applied tie pieces. To begin, I chose a color group of four ties. A spectacular Hermès tie printed with a feather motif became the theme and inspiration for the garment. The other ties in this group included one with a small, spaced geometric motif and two with classic narrow stripes.

I like to combine fabrics that contrast with each other in texture and color. Given the thin, smooth, and often shiny tie

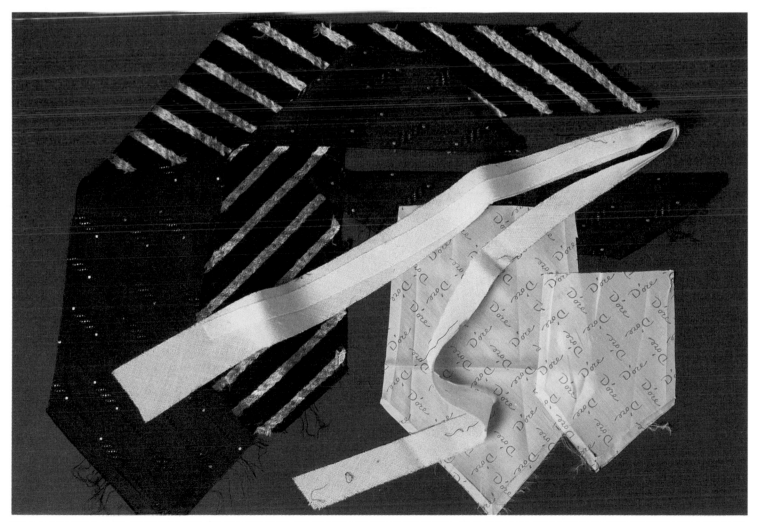

When you take a tie apart for the fabric (above), you'll often find that it is made from three pieces of fabric (brown with striped back), lining for both tips (right), and interfacing (yellow). A tie's front section can be a generous 10 in. wide.

fabrics, I wanted a base fabric that was thicker, rougher, and duller, so I purchased a deep blue polyester shantung with a heavy slub. A beige raw silk side panel that continues along the under sleeve provides a strong color contrast. To avoid interrupting the side panel's dramatic curved seamline, I used a kimono sleeve, which has no armscye seam.

To ensure that the base fabric would support the tie pieces without distorting, I completely underlined the garment with a thin cotton broadcloth. Because the garment sections where the ties would be applied were flat, I could arrange and rearrange the tie pieces with the garment section flat on the floor. I placed the bias tie strips diagonally at hip level on the side panels, applying them by strip piecing. The unanticipated result was that the stripes met at right angles at the side seams. I also used tie pieces for a narrow bias collar and for shoulder epaulets that imitate tie ends. Working on this first garment I discovered my love for braids and metallic trims, which has persisted throughout the series.

Curves and templates

A more difficult garment is one that is not underlined and whose tie pieces are not all linear strips. My fascination with Korean costume led to such a garment, a suit (shown in the right-hand photo on the facing page) based on the *chogore*, a Korean jacket characterized by striking underarm decorations, sleeve-hem trim, and collar. Koreans use red often in their clothing, and one of the color groups of ties I had put together was predominantly red. In addition, a Pierre Cardin tie in this group had a large round design flanked by band motifs that looked very Oriental to me. For the suit, I decided to use a dark blue rayon shantung as a contrast to the red, orange, and rust colorations of the ties. I did not underline the suit because I decided that the jacket fabric alone could support the weight of the tie pieces and trimming decoration. I lined the jacket in red silk.

The curved shapes needed for the decorative underarm appliqués made from tie pieces proved a real challenge. Even though I made cardboard templates for each of these appliqués, the bias tie pieces persisted in stretching and twisting. I had to resew each pieced tie appliqué by hand several times before it looked satisfactory.

Pleats and insets

Once you've mastered using tie fabrics flat, you're ready to experiment with texture, such as pleats. My most challenging garment, "Egyptian Goddess" (photo on p. 48), has highlights of pleated ties and a bias-cut back. The ties in the color group are predominantly black (and near black) and gold. I had turquoise in mind for the garment fabrics as a striking contrast to the ties. I found a handwoven silk fabric of turquoise alternating with black in both warp and weft. Its thick, dull slub texture contrasts nicely with the ties, and its heavy weight supports the weight of the tie pieces. A washed silk charmeuse in bright turquoise brightens the handwoven silk and looks great with the ties. I decided to use the handwoven silk for a jacket and the silk charmeuse for pants and top to wear under the jacket.

Working out the garment shape—When you apply ties to areas that will curve around the body when the garment was worn, it helps to fit the tie pieces with the garment sections pinned to a dress form. Playing with the black and turquoise fabric on a dress form, I found that when the fabric was placed on the bias, the weave structure formed a chevron along the center-back seam. I wanted the jacket to have flare in the back to complement the bias cut and as a departure from the tubular shapes of the previous garments. The neck and shoulders seemed the best area for tie embellishment; applying pieces to the flared areas of the jacket would have stiffened the flare too much.

I deliberated at length whether to underline the jacket. On the one hand, underlining would inhibit the flare. On the other hand, I worried that the bias cut would stretch and also would not support the weight of the tie pieces in the shoulder area. After an unsuccessful try at underlining the jacket only in the decorated areas, I underlined the entire jacket. I feel I made the right decision.

Playing with a pleater—Inspired by textile artist Lois Ericson's work (see *Threads* No. 39, p. 32 for Ericson's pleated jackets), I began to think about using a pleater that I had purchased eight months earlier and not yet used. I experimented by pleating the small section of tie fabric that wraps around the neck. I loved the result. This pleated piece reminded me of a bird's wings, and from this came my inspiration for the garment. Egyptian goddesses are depicted with winged headdresses or wings attached to their arms.

The ties for this project included a near-black tie with a gold reverse side and a gold tie with a black reverse side, either side of which could be the "right" side. A very bold tie had a large-scale printed lattice motif of white and gold on a black ground. Its scale was so large, I wondered how it would look in the garment. The print motif was visible but muted on its reverse side.

I pleated the largest tie section of the lattice motif fabric first. Controlling the bias fabric in the pleater took some practice, but it was exciting to see how the large lattice motif broke up when pleated and became less overpowering visually. I decided I liked the reverse side best.

Once I had removed the piece from the pleater, I had to control the side edges of the pleats so the pleats would stay in place. I traced a tissue paper copy of the upper part of the jacket-back pattern (right and left halves). I centered the pleated tie section on this paper pattern and machine basted the side edges of the pleats in place, stitching through both fabric and tissue paper pattern. Then I gently removed the tissue paper.

This pleated tie section fit perfectly centered on the upper back of the jacket. To break up the lattice pattern even more, I folded and stitched the down-facing pleats up along the center back.

I also pleated the solid gold and near-black ties. Pleating the tie pieces greatly reduced their length. To extend them, I split each tie's long sections in half lengthwise, producing two long and very narrow strips. Pleating these narrow bias pieces seemed harder to do than pleating the wider section had been.

I added two of these pleated sections along the sides of the center-back pleated piece, putting the wider ends at the shoulders, to reflect the triangular shape of the center pleated section. I let the outer edges remain free so that the strips would shape around the shoulder blades. The pleats also looked more three dimensional and winglike this way. I added pleated strips of the turquoise silk next to these tie strips.

Finishing the free edges of all these pleated strips concerned me. I felt that a rolled hem would probably be too bulky, but that a serged edge might work. I experimented with a spool of variegated metallic thread and set the serger for a rolled hem, but did not adjust the tension. Instead of rolling the fabric, the serger produced a very narrow serged edge that was just right. The edge wasn't bulky and it pressed nicely.

Before edge finishing all the pleated strips, I cut the free edges straight to eliminate the unevenness caused by the pleating. Serging opened the pleats, so I had to re-press them. I added several narrow trims and hand sewed all the pleated sections and trims to the jacket.

Linear pieces of bias lie fabric on the side of a garment, as on "Turkoman Ties"—worn by the author, above—are easy to apply. Curved pieces in contoured areas, as on the underarm panels on "Chogore," at right, require use of a template. (Photo above by Roger Schreiber; photo at right by Susan Kahn)

Turning to the front—The jacket front for "Egyptian Goddess" did not fall into place nearly as easily as the back had. Along one side of the front, I used an unpleated piece of the face side of the large-scale lattice motif so that both faces would appear on the jacket. To balance this strong pattern on the other side of the jacket, I stitched grosgrain ribbon in a zigzag pattern to a piece of the solid gold-colored fabric.

I folded the remaining two long, pleated strips—one near-black fabric reversing to gold and one gold reversing to near-black—in half so that each strip showed both faces. I put one strip on each side of the jacket front and added pleated sections of the turquoise silk charmeuse. Then I carefully hand sewed all the pleated sections into place, along

with some trims. Finally, I finished constructing the jacket.

The combination of the bias-cut back and the flared cut made determining the hemline of the jacket a near nightmare. My husband, my son, and a sewing comrade all assisted in pinning and basting the hem over and over again. Still not satisfied, I dug up a strip of horsehair braid and sewed it inside the hem to support the flare. This addition gave the hem the body it needed. Now I was satisfied. I added final touches of coins and yarn tassels, tied in place with turquoise cords.

Although I have had years of sewing experience, I still had to develop new and special techniques for each project. I learned what worked by trial and error. Allowing time for experimentation and not being discouraged by having to redo

something is critical to creative and involved projects such as these. I probably spent more time ripping and redoing than I spent doing the first time. Of course, some parts seemed to fall into place *almost* effortlessly.

Frequently I find myself thinking about other garment design possibilities with neckties. The ideas seem endless. Using Dad's neckties makes these garments very special to me. Wearing the outfits gives me the sense that he is with me and that he's pleased with what I've done with his ties. □

Nancy Bryant wrote about pattern grading in "Off-the-Chart Sizes," Threads No. 29, p. 58. She is an associate professor teaching apparel design courses at Oregon State University in Corvallis, OR.

Animating Appliqué
Free-motion embroidery adds control

by Sharee Dawn Roberts

Sharee Dawn Roberts adds realism to her appliquéd designs by painting in the details with machine embroidery on top of carefully selected fabrics. Her llama features appliqués of mohair teddy-bear fur. The basket is made from a grasscloth wallpaper remnant, and the passenger lifts out when the skirt on which the llama lives is cleaned.

When I discovered fabric, my life as an artist changed forever. I loved the textures, the feel of slubby cotton and satiny silk. I put away my paints and taught myself machine appliqué so I could add this tactile quality to the designs I was sketching from nature. But appliquéd shapes, however beautiful, always seemed stylized and graphic. I wanted my images of birds and flowers to come to life.

Then I saw some thread-painted pictures, made entirely with machine embroidery. Here was the detailed, painterly effect I sought for my designs. Soon I was thread-painting shaded flowers, furry animals, and even realistic people. But something was still missing. I had merely replaced brush strokes with thread and had eliminated the most appealing component, the fabric.

Finally it hit me. Why not appliqué my designs using the fabrics I loved, then add realism by thread-painting on top of the fabric? I soon developed the technique I call shaded appliqué, and after refining it for a couple of years, I finally feel confident that I can successfully interpret the images in my head, like the llama at left, with fabric and thread. My shaded designs are even supple enough to work on wearables.

The process isn't complicated; there are three main parts: drawing and transfering the design, appliquéing the shapes in place, then shading them. The shading and appliqué are done with free-motion machine embroidery (the feed dog is disengaged) for maximum flexibility and control. It helps to feel comfortable with drawing, but besides a good collection of colored embroidery threads and a zigzag sewing machine, the main ingredient you need is a willingness to practice the skills involved. I'll describe my process step by step and give some advice for shading realistically, but first let's look at the necessary supplies and talk about free-motion embroidery skills.

Tools and materials

With few exceptions, you should be able to find what you need locally, but mail-order sources are listed on p. 55.

Thread—Machine embroidery thread definitely gives the best results, both for appliqué and shading. I much prefer 100% rayon thread, as its finer weight, low twist, and high luster produce the most appealing stitches. Some familiar brand names are Sulky (I use the thinner size 40), Mez Alcazar, Madeira, and Natesh. All-cotton machine-embroidery thread (such as DMC) is also very satisfactory, even though it's not as glossy and doesn't fill in as easily. Regardless of which top threads I'm using, I always use cotton embroidery thread in the bobbin (either white if I'm working on light fabrics or black for very dark ones) because it's thin and won't add bulk.

The most important consideration is to use just the right colors to match the fabric you're appliquéing, and to create effective shading, so I'll even use a dressmakers' thread instead of embroidery thread, if necessary. The easiest way to get a good match is to buy your threads first, then find fabrics that match.

Fabric and batting—You can use any fabric with my technique, but I tend to use mostly lightweight, silky fabrics because the stitches blend in better and the final result is more appropriate for wearables. I preshrink any natural fibers, and I machine wash and drip dry, or dry-clean garments made from these. When I use batting, I prefer either Hobbs Thermore or Fairfield Processing's Cotton Classic because they're so thin; they're widely available at quilters' suppliers.

Fusible web—Fusible web is a layer of fusible adhesive on a paper backing. When you fuse it to fabric, then peel off the paper, you can then fuse that fabric to something else. I use it to attach my appliqué shapes to the background fabric before stitching them down. Pellon's Wonder-Under is the brand I'm most familiar with. It's sold at most fabric stores, usually with the interfacing. Similar products are called Magic Fuse, Transfer Fusing, and Trans-Web.

Fusible stabilizer—This product is temporarily fused to the wrong side of the background fabric to stabilize it during free-motion embroidery; you tear it away afterwards. It eliminates the need for an embroidery hoop you'd have to shift to cover a large design. I use it for appliqué, but it's tedious to remove from under

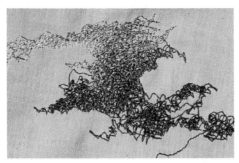

Up close, and over a contrasting background, Roberts' shading stitches are revealed to be mere squiggles.

thread painting, and makes the final fabric stiff, so for shading I prefer the hoop.

Stabilizers are sold at many sewing centers where machine appliqué and embroidery classes are held; one brand is called Iron-On Tear-Away. Polycoated freezer wrapping paper (sold in grocery stores—don't get the all-plastic kind) may be substituted; the polycoated side fuses to fabric just like the stabilizers, and it's less expensive.

Darning foot—This handy little foot holds stabilized fabric firmly against the needle plate so you can do free motion work without using a hoop. Many sewing machines come with a darning foot (the working end looks like a little ring or open rectangle), but they can also be purchased to fit any sewing machine.

Light box—I use this to transfer my designs to the stabilizer and fabric and to position cutout shapes accurately on the background fabric for appliquéing. It creates backlighting so that you can trace through nontransparent layers, like fabric. You can tape designs and fabric on large windows for a similar effect, but it's easier to work on a horizontal surface. Art supply stores sell professional models, but see *Threads*, No. 38, p. 12 for a way to make an inexpensive version.

Getting started

When you drop the feed dog on your machine and control the movement of the fabric under the needle by hand, you're doing free-motion work, so called because this way you can move the fabric in any direction as you stitch. I use two variations: shading and appliqué.

Free-motion shading—The shading I do is similar to thread painting: I set my machine to straight stitch and color with thread just as I would color with a pencil if I were drawing; I just move the fabric instead of the needle. It's like drawing by moving paper under a stationary pencil.

There's no right or wrong way to thread-paint. Some people color in tiny cross hatches, some make loops or circles, and some people use broad strokes. I make squiggles, as you can see at left, but everyone's style is different, and so is the appearance of their work. I encourage you to develop your own style, based on what you're most comfortable with.

You'll need to learn how to move the fabric smoothly in any direction, following your design, while controlling the size of your stitches. If you move the fabric faster, you'll get longer stitches; if you press your foot petal faster, you'll get shorter stitches. Like all hand/eye coordination skills, control comes with practice. As you learn to relax, your stitching will become more consistent.

To practice, you can remove the foot and use a hoop, as I do when I'm shading (the fabric is held at the bottom of the hoop, next to the needle plate), or use a darning foot and fusible stabilizer on the back, as I do for the appliqué. Drop the feed dog, loosen the top tension so the top thread is pulled slightly to the wrong side, slip the fabric underneath, and lower the foot lever, even if you're not using a foot. If you don't, the tension won't engage, and big loops will form underneath. This is a common mistake, so don't be discouraged if it happens to you; just clip the loops and start over. Hold the threads as you make the first stitch. Start making little circles, and side-to-side strokes, then try stitching your name, or simple shapes, and experiment with the machine speed as you play.

Free-motion appliqué—Machine appliqué traditionally is worked in a close satin stitch using an appliqué foot with the feed dog engaged. You need to pivot often when traveling around tight curves and to taper the stitch for sharp points, so it's very difficult to appliqué intricate designs. Also, the mechanical satin stitch that this produces around the edges interferes with the design. When I drop the feed dog and work free-motion, with my machine set for a medium-width (2.5mm to 3mm) zigzag stitch, I can slide around those tiny curves and sharp points instead of pivoting, controlling the width and angle of the satin stitches for much more realistic designs.

With your machine set up like this, zigzag stitches will appear when you move the fabric forward or backward; as in thread painting, you are controlling the stitch length. The zigzags will form smooth satin stitches when you get the hang of moving the fabric steadily, as the machine runs at a constant speed. When you move sideways, you'll be forming what I call side stitch, and when you move diagonally, you'll form a slanted satin stitch. You can see the effect in the photo on p. 52.

You'll find that as you sew sideways, the stitch formed will not be wide enough to secure an edge of fabric. You'll have to move back and forth slightly, "darning" the edges until the stitching is wide enough to cover the raw edge. Again, with practice, this side stitching will blend smoothly into the satin stitches. Before you try covering a fabric edge, practice just making smooth satin and side stitches and blending between them, on a single layer of fabric. Then draw a shape on the fabric and practice covering the line.

Designing the appliqué

When I'm designing for clothing, I start by machine basting a test garment out of sheets of newsprint, instead of muslin, so I can sketch ideas on the actual garment shape, or trace completed designs in place, using my light box. I prefer shaped garments, so there are usually lots of seams and darts, but I sketch right over them. They don't interfere with the appliqué. When I'm doing the actual stitching, I do everything I can on the separate pieces before they're sewn together first, then do the designs that cross seams after they're attached.

Right from the start, I draw my designs so they can be easily cut out in fabric. I make a detailed line drawing that outlines each shape that will be a separate piece and includes any interior lines that

I'll want to cover with satin stitch. I add the basic outline of any thread-painted details, like eyes, but I don't include any indications of where I'll add shading; that'll come later.

Getting the design on fabric

I put my outline drawing face down on the light box as shown in the drawing on the facing page, then cut a piece of fusible stabilizer the same size as the pattern piece and place it fusible side down over my design. With a fine-point black marker, I trace the entire design in the position I want it. When the stabilizer is fused under the background fabric and it's put right side up on the light box, the design will serve as a position guide for the appliquéd pieces as well as a stabilizer for the appliquéing.

Next I trace the design onto the fusible web, once again fusible side down over the face-down outline, but this time I trace each shape that will be a separate piece of fabric separately, including all detail lines. Wherever the shapes will overlap, I extend the outline on the underlayer by ⅛ in.

Next I cut the shapes roughly out of the web and fuse them to the wrong side of each appliqué fabric—grain is unimportant—then trim them carefully along the traced line. On the light box I trace to the top of the fabric any internal lines that I'll want to cover with satin stitch, using the black permanent marker. If the design is complex, I'll number the pieces on the paper backing.

I put the background face up on the light box and remove the paper backing

from each appliqué shape, then position them, overlapping where necessary. I've found that if I first put a layer of 1-in. foam rubber over the light box, I can tack each shape into place with the iron tip right on the light box, before carefully fusing them at the ironing board. The design is now ready to stitch.

Appliquéing the design

To prepare the machine for free-motion appliqué on the stabilized background, I drop the feed dog, put on the darning foot, and decrease the top tension slightly. I use a size 80/12 needle, unless the fabrics are thicker than normal. For most appliqué shapes I'll use a 2.5mm zigzag width, but if the shapes are tiny, I'll reduce the width accordingly.

The direction that you stitch in relation to the design is critical. For the smoothest result, curves should be satin stitched and points should be side stitched. Line your needle swing up with any tiny curve or sharp point *before* you start stitching. Think of your needle as forming a horizontal line as it swings back and forth.

After all the appliqué is completed and you are satisfied with your design, remove all fusible stabilizer from the back, before adding the shading stitches. Large areas tear away easily, and I remove the tiny bits of paper left in points and corners with tweezers.

Understanding shading

To create convincing shading in embroidery, you need a good understanding of how value creates depth. The basics are

From left to right, a shaded design starts out as cutout shapes fused to a background. The shapes are machine appliquéd in place with free-motion satin stitch in matching thread, then shaded with graduated thread colors. It's finished with a thin thread outline around each shape, and a bit of embellishment with metallic threads.

Roberts follows a careful value drawing to establish where to work her machine-embroidered shading. Once the drawing is done, she can use it as a guide to shade the design in any color.

simple: Light values appear to advance while dark values look like they're receding. In other words, the part of a design that's closest will be a lighter value than the part farthest away. Also, when areas of a design overlap, the part underneath will be in shadow while the area on top will be lighter.

It's easiest to think in terms of black, white, and gray when you're planning a shaded design. This way you can plan values before you plan colors. I use gray colored pencils (PrismaColors come in graduated shades of gray) to color in my shades on a copy of my original design. I'll stitch these areas of shading with corresponding values of thread.

I start by imagining a light source. If I can think of my design as being lighted from a particular place, it's easier for me to determine where to add my lightest values. I simply draw a sun somewhere on my sketch (it can be anywhere: off to one side, above, or below) and then I think of the rays coming from the sun to my design. Highlights will be the areas of the design closest to this light source. With my lightest gray pencil, I color in areas that I imagine are highlighted by my sun, and those areas of the design that are overlapping others, like a stem in front of a leaf.

Next, I switch to my darkest pencil (usually black), and I color in the areas that I feel will be shaded: those that are the farthest from the light source, and those that are in the shadows.

After defining the highlights and the shades, I use middle values of gray to blend—darker grays to blend into the black, and lighter grays to blend into the highlighted areas. This drawing, like the one in the photo on the facing page, is a roadmap to guide me while I'm stitching.

The next step is the most critical: selecting the thread. Again, I think in terms of value as opposed to color. First of all, I consider the thread that I use to appliqué my design as my middle value, corresponding to the middle gray I use for blending. Then I carefully pick out values of that same color that are darker and lighter; I like to use at least four shades. All that's left is to color in with my sewing machine, matching the values in my drawing.

Shading the design

Shading on the machine is actually the easiest part of the process. Set up your machine as for the appliqué, but switch to straight stitch, remove the darning foot, and put the work in a 7-in. or 8-in. embroidery hoop.

I like to add the embroidery in the same sequence that I colored in the shades with my colored pencils: starting with the lightest value, then adding the darks, then blending with the medium shades. You can always add more of any shade after stepping back and evaluating your piece. You can even cover up stitches by embroidering over them with a different shade. Just remember that the embroidery is added only to shade your design and not to cover up the fabric. As you work, look at your design from a distance every once in a while; the values will stand out more when viewed from a few feet away.

For the finishing touches, I thread-paint with the color I used for the appliqué to further blend and soften the shading, then add a straight-stitch outline to each shape, in a dark shade of the appliqué color. This seems to define the shapes and add dimension, and is even more effective if there's batting underneath. Sometimes I'll add other accents, like the trailing vines in the photo on the facing page, by flipping the work over and embroidering with a heavy decorative thread in the bobbin case.

When the design is completed, there may be a few puckers in the work. I simply place my design right side down on a padded ironing board and spray it with a fine mist of water. Then I smooth away the puckers with my hands and carefully press with a dry iron. □

Sharee Dawn Roberts teaches machine embroidery classes across the country. Her appliquéd garments appear regularly in the annual Fairfield Fashion Show.

Sources

English's Sewing Machine Co.
7001 Benton Rd.
Paducah, KY 42003
(800) 525-7845
Mez Alcazar rayon thread, DMC cotton thread, stabilizers, Wonder-Under, and darning feet.

Aardvark Adventures
PO Box 2449, Dept. TH
Livermore, CA 94551
(800) 388-ANTS(2687)
Lots of embroidery threads including Natesh rayon thread, and other embellishments. Catalog $2, applicable to first purchase.

Treadleart
25834 Narbonne Ave.
Lomita, CA 90717
(800) 327-4222
Sulky and Madeira rayon thread, DMC and Metrosene cotton threads, Iron-On Tear-Away, Wonder-Under, darning feet, and hoops. Catalog $3.

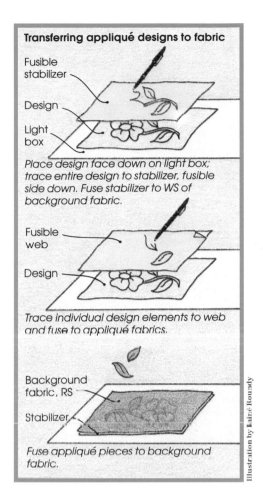

Transferring appliqué designs to fabric

Fusible stabilizer

Design

Light box

Place design face down on light box; trace entire design to stabilizer, fusible side down. Fuse stabilizer to WS of background fabric.

Fusible web

Design

Trace individual design elements to web and fuse to appliqué fabrics.

Background fabric, RS

Stabilizer

Fuse appliqué pieces to background fabric.

Illustration by Laine Roundy

Free-motion thread-painted appliqué is flexible enough to use on all types of garments. (Photo by Glenn Hall)

Pattern-Printing Primer
The sewer's guide to rubber-stamping on fabric

by Carol Voulkos

design sources are everywhere; anything can inspire when your eye and imagination join forces. Recognizing the many possibilities, however, can be as frustrating as it is liberating. Where do you begin? One technique that designers have for escaping this blur of endless choices is to start with a single, humble, familiar visual element and then try to make something wonderful and new from it. What happens when you merely repeat the element? How many ways can you combine it with itself to create new elements, new designs? What if you start with just a letter? What if you use the whole alphabet? The only rule is that it must be fun.

I've had so much fun with this idea of repeating simple shapes that I've been designing with it for years, using all kinds of techniques, from appliqué to embroidery. But when I stumbled upon a rubber-stamp alphabet and started stamping designs on fabric, I knew I'd found the easiest way yet to open the door to surface design. I invariably use my best designs to embellish simple garments, so I've included here a useful vest pattern and a description of how I construct a stamped version.

Introducing the rubber stamp

Artists have definitely discovered the rubber stamp. Ready-made stamps are perfect for exploring repetition and for playing with instant images, and it's quick and inexpensive to have a stationery store make a stamp from your own black-and-white line drawing. A whole community of rubber-stamping artists has sprung up, complete with companies that produce stamps of every type just for their decorative and expressive possibilities. There's even a regular magazine, *Rubberstampmadness* (Box 6585, Ithaca, NY 14851; sample issue, $3) edited by Rubberta Sperling, which should tell you how sober and restrained this subculture is.

Once the bug has bitten you, you'll find rubber-stamp catalogs seductive, and stamp collecting addictive. You can invest a lot of money once you start red-penciling their offerings. For an inexpensive start, look around in drugstore and super-market toy sections. You'll be surprised at how many rubber stamps are made for children. I've picked up alphabets, animals, and a wide variety of simple images for very little money. You can even make your own stamps by cutting shapes into plastic erasers with a razor knife.

Taking proper care of your stamps is important. I keep mine in small cardboard boxes on their sides, not on the image. I cover each box with plain bond paper and stamp on the lid with each stamp that's inside the box. This saves a lot of time when I'm frantically looking for "that stamp." I store the boxes in a cool, dark place; sunlight will ruin them quickly.

I've often read that you should never use an oil-based ink on rubber stamps, as the ink will corrode rubber. However, since I stamp on fabric, I want my creations to be washable, so I use waterproof, oil-based laundry ink. I keep a box of facial tissues nearby, and I wipe each stamp after every stamping. After several years, I haven't noticed any damage. Whatever kind of ink you use, I suggest that you wipe the stamps every time you stamp them. Occasionally I thoroughly clean each stamp with soapy water or Windex and an old toothbrush. Keeping the stamps clean is the only way to keep the edges of the designs unclogged and the printing sharp.

You can special-order laundry ink, in black only, from most stationery stores. It's smelly and should be used in a well-ventilated room. This ink is very colorfast; I once soaked a mistake in a solution of Clorox and water for several days, and that print didn't budge. I use uninked pads (felt pads are better than foam rubber) and store them upside down to keep the ink on the surface. You can wet the pad with 2 or 3 tbsp. of ink. Cover your work surface, and wear old clothes when you work with this stuff.

Many colored stamp pads are available, and they're fine for paper stamping, but I doubt if they'll launder. New products are coming out all the time, so maybe soon we'll have laundry-fast stamping colors that are bright, fresh, and interesting. In the meantime you can use any fabric paint and mix colors to your taste. I make my own disposable pads for paint because it doesn't store well. Cough-drop tins make good pad holders. To make the pads, I soak several layers of cut-to-fit white felt in tepid water and wring them almost dry. I cover the damp felt with a layer of old cotton sheeting and stitch it tight all around. Then I pour some fabric paint onto the damp pad, work the paint into the felt with the back of a spoon, and use the pad immediately.

If your stamp has a lot of detail and isn't printing well or is too big for a pad, you can get good, if slow, results by rolling out the ink or paint on a hard, smooth surface and transferring it to the stamp with a brayer, a hard rubber roller sold by artist-supply stores. Or, you can load the stamp by rubbing it with a permanent marker. This has the advantage of letting you color different parts of the stamp differently for multicolor images from a single stamping.

Stamping out a vest

Let's get into a surface-design project. The vests in the photo on the facing page come from the simple pattern that I've provided on p. 58. It's a one-piece shape that lies flat, so it's an ideal canvas for a single, big rubber-stamp design. If you want to use your own pattern, see if you can eliminate the side seams; it's a lot easier to keep the design flowing if the front and the back are one piece. If you use my pattern, make a muslin first so that you'll be able to adjust

The simple shape of Carol Voulkos's vest makes it an ideal backdrop for her graphic surface design, which is entirely concocted of repeated letter shapes. Rubber stamps make the design process easy and spontaneous.

the length and slope of the shoulder seams to match your figure.

Any smooth-surfaced cotton or poly blend will do to print on. A rough, loosely woven fabric will cloud your stamped image. Sale-priced sheets and pillowcases are wonderful sources for surface-design yardage. They launder beautifully and come in good colors. Whatever you use, *always* preshrink it.

I trace my pattern onto the outer fabric with a blue wash-out marker (available at sewing stores), making sure that it's on grain. I allow for seams only at the shoulder because I finish the other edges with bias binding. If I want to emphasize the outline with a stamped border, I draw guidelines inside the traced outline, showing the stitching line for the bias tape, and the inside edge of the border design.

With the outlines established, but before I do any cutting, I start stamping my design, using the blank space outside the pattern for tests. The fabric is free to move, so I can stamp from any angle. I keep plenty of typing paper nearby for working out my ideas, and if I'm working on a border, I start with that. A border makes a design look planned and definite regardless of what

goes on inside it. I make the neckline border slightly wider than the armhole borders, and I usually make each armhole border a little different; it's more interesting that way.

I usually begin stamping the main design in an underarm area so I can get warmed up for the focal points—the backs and fronts. No matter how sure I am about my intended design, I always find myself improvising and being surprised as I go along. The design happens right before your eyes, and all sorts of things start to occur as you stamp, urging you to develop them. Each stamped image is always a little different from the last, and rarely exactly where you want it, because it's hard to stamp each time in the very same way.

It's helpful when you're lining up images if you can see the edge of some part of the stamp's image from the side. To get the clearest images, I put a thick, smooth magazine under the fabric where I'm stamping for a good printing surface, but these inconsistencies are part of the pleasure of stamped designs. Sometimes the rubber backing at the corners of a stamp will print along with the design. This looks awful,

but you can eliminate it by trimming the corners with a razor knife.

I think of every design as an experiment. If you plan something and make a mistake, instead of panicking, think about it for a while. By changing your original idea and going along with what you've done, you can usually come up with an entirely new approach. So plunge right in; go for spontaneity over polish. It's the nature of the medium.

Horizontal rows of type are obviously just the beginning with alphabet stamps. By adding a slight curve to your rows as you stamp each letter, you can end up with beautifully free-flowing swirls. After going through stripes and swirls, I moved on to small enclosed areas of repeated stampings, like the harlequin pattern in the photo on p. 57. I blocked out the diamonds with strips of tape (transparent or masking tape works well) to create clean edges. Why not reproduce quilt blocks with stamped textures instead of pieced fabrics?

Consider creating texture and pattern with words instead of repeated letters. Their meaning can be part of the design, can tell a story, or can just form unreadable patterns. Text can be horizontal, vertical, me-

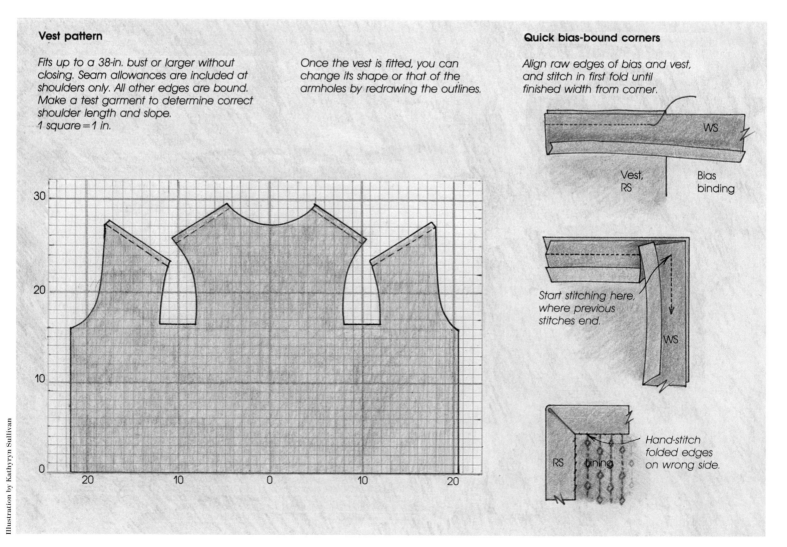

Vest pattern

Fits up to a 38-in. bust or larger without closing. Seam allowances are included at shoulders only. All other edges are bound. Make a test garment to determine correct shoulder length and slope.
1 square = 1 in.

Once the vest is fitted, you can change its shape or that of the armholes by redrawing the outlines.

Quick bias-bound corners

Align raw edges of bias and vest, and stitch in first fold until finished width from corner.

WS

Vest, RS   Bias binding

Start stitching here, where previous stitches end.

WS

Hand-stitch folded edges on wrong side.

RS   Lining

Illustration by Kathryn Sullivan

andering, in blocks, run together without spacing, etc. Inspect my designs for ideas that you can develop into your own. If you get into alphabets, the more sizes and styles you acquire, the more possibilities you'll have for exploration.

Machine quilting and finishing

When I'm finished stamping my design, I lay the stamped fabric face down on my cutting table and cover it with a matching piece of quilt batting. I prefer Thermolamb. I cover this with a lining fabric (choose something interesting), right side up, and pin the layers together. Then I baste the whole thing, every 5 or 6 in., both horizontally and vertically so nothing can shift around. This is critical if you're going to quilt it. If I've chosen a silky polyester lining (it feels so good!), I baste the stamped fabric and the batting together first and then baste the lining to that. Even though you're still working with uncut rectangles, it's much easier to handle this way.

You don't have to quilt this fabric sandwich, but it will hang better, wash better, and last longer if you do. I do it all by machine. Make a sample of your layered fabrics to test the pressure and tension settings on your machine. If you're just sewing straight lines, you're ready to go, but if you want curves, or if you're following shapes in the design, lower your feed dogs, but keep the presser foot on, as I'm doing in the photo at right; I use my all-purpose straight/zigzag foot.

I can hear some of you slumping to the floor at the thought of all this, but because your sandwich is very thick and securely basted, guiding your work around the borders and interior shapes isn't as difficult as you might think. Always start quilting from the center out to the edges and from the middle to the top and bottom. Grasp your work firmly with both hands. Start slowly; it doesn't take much time to work out the right speed, feel, and rhythm.

With all the layers together and all the stitching completed, now and *only* now do I cut out the garment. This way, everything will be exactly the same size. Next, I remove the basting and sew the shoulder seams, through outer fabric and Thermolamb, right sides together, then through the lining, wrong sides together. I finish these seam allowances by hand-felling one allowance over the other, usually toward the front.

To finish the edges, I make bias tape (½ in. finished) with those Clover tape markers available in most notions departments. I prefer black cotton broadcloth for making my own bias tape. It gives the jacket a definite finish, like a frame. But the choice is yours—solid colors, prints, stripes, polka-

With the stamped fabric layered on top of Thermolamb batting and a lining fabric and all securely basted, Voulkos drops the feed dogs on her machine (but leaves on the presser foot) and quilts in all directions around her stamped motifs.

dots, whatever you like. Some people are good at stitching in the ditch, but I feel more comfortable stitching the tape on the right side with the sewing machine, right sides and edges together, folding the tape over the edge, and finishing on the wrong side with a slipstitch. See the drawing at right on the facing page for a simple method for going around outside corners. For inside corners, just keep the work in the machine and pivot when you come to the corner, needle down. You can arrange the fold in the tape when you slipstitch it down later. For a nice smooth edge to fold the bias over, I run a line of stitching around the entire vest just inside the cutting line before I cut it out.

Garments that are made in this way can be hand-washed. Always make a test swatch first. I have silks dry-cleaned, but cottons and blends don't even need pressing, especially if you've done a reasonable amount of quilting.

Other possibilities

If starting with a vest is intimidating, try a smaller project first: pot holder, book cover, place mat, pillowcase, tote bag, quilt block, etc. It's not necessary to make your own garment. I've picked up ready-made vests and stamped them. You have to select with care, making sure that the fabric is smooth enough to accept stamping and that there aren't too many pockets or double thicknesses of fabric to inhibit the stamping.

T-shirts are easy to stamp. Put a piece of light cardboard inside the shirt so you don't ink through to the back. If the cardboard is big enough, it will also help keep the knit stretched, but experiment with stamping on stretched knits. You can completely change the stamped image. I've read about one adventurous soul who rubber-stamped her panty hose! □

Carol Voulkos designs and teaches in San Francisco, CA.

The Incredible, Reversible, One-Technique Jacket

Machine quilting as a construction method

by Bird Ross

a friend once said to me, "Make your work look as good on the inside as it does on the outside." Little did I realize then what an impact that advice would have on the things I make now, almost 10 years later. My work, like the tops and hats on the facing page, has no right or wrong side; it's double-sided, completely reversible, and I get to play with at least twice as much color and pattern as I would if I were making only one-sided pieces.

I construct each of my garments without any of the usual construction techniques. They're entirely formed out of the randomly stitched machine quilting that I use to hold together the three layers: inside, outside, and a stabilizer in the middle. Using only the forward and reverse straight stitch on the most basic sewing machine (I have an old Singer Featherweight), I can join sections, finish seams and edges, and create texture and pattern, all at once. As I quilt the layers of fabric, I'm creating both sides of the jacket at the same time. I'm also transforming the colors and patterns of the commercial yardage by overlaying them with thread, and changing the effect of the cloth's original design by juxtaposing it with new patterns, as I add new fabrics.

There are three main steps to the process. First I choose a pattern and adapt it to my requirements. Then I select the two fabrics that I'll use inside and out in addition to an inner fabric, cut them out in identical layers, and machine quilt them together, covering the fabric with random lines of colored quilting. Finally, I

Bird Ross reinvents the garment by discarding everything she ever learned about sewing (well, almost). Her completely reversible, machine-washable pieces are constructed entirely with machine quilting. (Photo by Susan Kahn)

form the seams, finish the edges, and add pockets if I want them, in each case by machine quilting single layers of contrasting fabrics over the layered garment pieces. The process uses lots of thread!

I use the same techniques to create baskets, as well as hats, vests, and neckties. Machine quilting gives a whole new look and feel to the original fabric, and the juxtaposition of the patterns adds another intriguing element to the creation of garments. Here's how it's done.

Simplifying the pattern

I begin my garments with commercial patterns. I make sure to start with one whose basic shape excites me, since I'll be paring it down to the bare essentials. The patterns that work best are simple and uncluttered to begin with, without separate sleeve pieces. My jackets aren't meant to be fitted, and because of their bulk and relative stiffness (about the same as any heavily quilted garment), they'll be more comfortable if they're slightly oversized. If you've chosen a pattern that you've used before, the fit will be slightly less subtle because of the bulk and because you'll be eliminating some of the seams.

First adjust the pattern for size, then look for seams that you can do without. If the garment has a center-back seam, copy the pattern and tape the back pieces together to make a new pattern piece without the center seam, removing any shaping so the new pattern lies flat. You won't need any facings. I integrate separate collar pieces into the main pattern shape. If the sleeves have separate cuffs, simply lengthen the sleeves to incorporate the cuff length. I always add an extra two inches to each of the sleeves anyway to allow for shrinkage. It's easier to cut the length off later than it is to add length, and this way you can relax when you put the pieces in the washing machine. You

can use the pattern's patch pocket shapes when you make pockets later, or you can draw your own, but cut off any pockets that extend from the side seams.

Creating a new fabric

This technique lends itself to lots of variations, and the main variable is the feel and look of the new fabric you'll be creating by quilting layers. I've worked out some guidelines to help reduce your trial and error, but experimentation is part of the fun of the project, and I do lots of it. For a finished jacket with the least number of unpleasant surprises, it's vital that you make samples first so that you can check for color fastness and shrinkage. I usually make my jackets completely machine washable and dryable, but even if you plan to dry-clean yours, the layering and quilting process can cause major transformations, including shrinkage.

Making samples—Once you've chosen your fabrics, or better yet *before* you have any idea what fabrics you ultimately want to use in your jacket, cut out some sample squares and try the process. If you don't make any samples first, your final garment will be a very risky business.

Start by cutting eight 8-in. squares. Use a variety of fabrics including novelty fabrics, silks, cottons of various weights, transparent fabrics, anything you like. Pair these fabrics for a total of four back-to-back squares wrong sides together as they would be in a finished garment.

Then choose a fabric for the middle layer. This is a stabilizer that allows you to use any type of fabric on either side of it. It adds needed body if you want to use two very lightweight fabrics, and it helps balance very different fabrics.

The stabilizer also adds bulk, which is why I like to wash the layers as many as three times before the jacket is complete. This gives it a more relaxed feel. I use

To finish edges (left), *Ross positions fabric squares over the edge and stitches half the square down. Then she folds the un-stitched half over the edge and stitches it down from the other side.* **Shoulder seams** *are overlapped, then covered on one side with a contrast strip of fabric, which is then zigzagged (above). On the other side, contrast fabric squares are zigzagged over the seam.*

lightweight upholstery fabrics, such as chintzes, as stabilizers. They're all-cotton, 60 in. wide, and generally are available at larger fabric stores as bolt ends for very little money. Make sure the fabric won't bleed and that it's either a pale solid or a subtle print that won't show through.

Unless you're looking for the maximum texture (as described below), prewash this middle layer fabric. Cut four 8-in. squares and sandwich one between each of the four pairs of outer fabrics. Pin the three layers together using as few pins as you feel comfortable with. When you sew your jacket, you can use as many pins as you like to keep things from shifting. But on the sample, the fewer pins, the less to keep track of once you begin sewing.

Doing the manual zigzag—Remember when you were first learning to sew and you were told always to use the same color bobbin thread as the top thread, and that the thread should match your fabric? Well, forget those rules and pick your two favorite colors, ones that will complement, contrast, or conflict with the fabric in your first set of squares. Put one color on top and the other in your bobbin, and set your machine to sew a medium-length straight stitch.

Place your needle anywhere you want within the square. Lower the presser foot and begin by sewing several inches in one direction, then put your machine in reverse and sew backwards for several inches, without going over the original stitches, then again forwards and then again backwards. You're now doing what I call the "manual zigzag." It may take some practice before you get used to doing it with your machine. If yours is a machine

that requires you to hold the reverse button down as you sew in reverse, then practice until you feel comfortable holding the button and manipulating the fabric at the same time.

Do the manual zigzag randomly all over your 8-in. square. Try not to fill in any one area of your square more than another. Remove the pins as you get to them. Move all around the square with your machine, using just as many reverse as forward stitches. Don't be in a hurry. Think of these stitches as paint or colored pencil strokes, and add lots of color.

Sew all four samples separately, adding as much color as you like. You won't be completely covering the square with thread, but sew a greater concentration of stitches in some squares than others so that you'll get an idea of the various effects. You can try synthetic as well as cotton thread, and try mixing them in top and bobbin. Try some metallic threads. I usually change threads three times on top and bobbin before I'm through.

Once you've completed the samples, toss them in the washing machine, and then into the dryer, unless any of them include fabrics you wouldn't ordinarily put in the machine or if you don't intend to wash them once they're made into a jacket. Once they're totally dry, iron them flat.

Some of your squares will have lots of texture. Notice how much your squares have or haven't shrunk. Some of that has to do with the fiber content, but a lot of it has to do with the number of stitches you put in your fabric: more stitches, more shrinkage. Notice, too, how unsquare some of the pieces may have become, or how different layers in the square may

have raveled or shrunk more than other layers. Trim the edges as little as possible to straighten them.

The changes that take place in your samples will tell you how to prepare the fabric before you begin on your jacket. For example, if the fit of your garment would be spoiled if it shrinks, then pre-wash and dry all of your fabric layers twice to shrink the fabric as much as possible before you do any of the cutting and sewing. These preliminary washings will *not* keep the fabric from shrinking entirely because adding the stitches later will cause more shrinkage, but it helps.

Covering the edges—The next step for your sample is to cut about thirty-five 2-in. squares of contrasting fabric for each sample square. A rotary cutter and straightedge will be a big help. Position the squares to your right as you sit at the machine. Pick up one square at a time, and lay the diagonal along the edge of the sample so that half of each little square falls off, as in the left-hand photo above, then sew it down with more manual zigzags. Move around the layered edges, laying down new little squares and overlapping the points about 1 in., and sewing only half of each square to the sample. The other half will be folded over later, wrapping around to finish the edge. It's a good idea to make some samples with curved edges, too, so you can practice finishing shapes like necklines and curved jacket openings.

Once you've gone completely around all of your edges, turn the sample over and sew down all the other halves of the little squares. Make sure you pull them flush to the edge of the sample. Don't pin

Machine quilting large pattern shapes cut from three layers of fabric requires a wide table, room to move, and a wide-armed grip on the fabric. A machine that can be set to sew in reverse frees both of Ross's hands for maximum control.

these down in advance; you'll want to manipulate them as you go. You can baste them all in place with a single row of stitches first. The corners will be bulky, so trim away any excess fabric from the 2-in. square as you fold.

Now put all the sample squares in the washer and dryer to check once more for shrinkage and squareness. Again, some of the texture and crookedness can be ironed out. Press the pieces just to see what happens. If you were happier with the texture before you did the pressing, just throw the pieces back in the washer and dryer.

Planning ahead—To control the final texture of your new fabric, try these ideas.

For the *most* texture and a soft, worn hand, use any combination of the following: Choose only natural fiber fabrics. Prewash only those fabrics which will shrink a great deal, like gauzes. Use fabrics which have different fiber contents; for example, you'll get a lot of texture if you sandwich two layers of cotton around a polyester middle layer because of the inconsistent shrinkage. If your thread content is different from your fiber content, you'll get more texture than if you use matching thread.

For *less* texture, use any combination of the following: Prewash all of your fabric before cutting. Use all synthetic fabrics. Sew with fewer manual zigzag stitches when you're sandwiching the layers together. All fabric layers and thread should have the same fiber content.

The more samples you make, the more discoveries you'll make, and the more questions you'll have answered before you get to the jacket. You should also feel

as comfortable sewing in reverse as you do going forward before you plunge into jacket making.

Sewing the jacket

Start by choosing your fabrics, both outer layers and the stabilizing layer. You can choose the edge fabric(s) when you get to that step.

You'll be cutting three layers at a time, so you'll need a big cutting surface. Lay the fabric out with the bottom layer face down. The middle layer can be either side up, but the top layer will be right side up. Pin the pattern pieces on top catching all three layers, and cut all the layers at once. Ideally, you'll have one pattern piece for the back and one pattern piece for the front, which you'll use twice, making sure you flip it over so you don't cut two left fronts.

Quilting the layers—Once they've been cut out, pin the three layers together thoroughly so that they will be ready for sewing. This takes a lot of pins on every 2 to 3 in. Perhaps you're wondering why I don't first sew the three layers of fabric together and then cut out the pattern pieces. You can do that; in fact, if you want to be absolutely sure you get no shrinkage in the garment, you might want to sew the layers together, wash and dry them, and then cut the pattern pieces out. However, you'll be using much more fabric, you'll have more waste once you cut out, and initially you'll be handling much bigger pieces of fabric at the machine.

Now you're ready to sew the layers together. Proceed with these pieces as you did with your sample squares. The fabric will be more cumbersome, and you can't

hold it the way you do for normal sewing. And instead of sewing a few inches before changing direction, you'll sew for about 6 to 8 in. before switching. Take your time and sew carefully. It will be tricky to keep everything flat. If you're having trouble, stop and put in more stabilizing pins. If you've put in too many pins and you're worrying about breaking your needle, take some out. But be sure to sew over the entire pattern piece.

It's important to have a consistent amount of stitching—heavy, medium, or light—within each piece, and the same consistency in all the pieces of a single garment. Otherwise you will get uneven puckering and shrinkage, and an irregular texture, which might lead to seams not matching, lengths being different, and so on. This first layer of thread is the most painstaking. You're fixing all of your layers together at this point. After this you'll be able to add as much thread and color as you want without having to worry about everything staying flat. I still get glitches where the fabric catches in a fold, but I just live with them.

Once you've finished with your first layer of thread, change your threads on the top and bottom and add other colors. I always sew a total of three layers of thread. After you've completed all the pattern pieces, wash them in hot water and throw them in the dryer, then give them a good steam pressing.

Making seams—The next step is to sew the pattern pieces together. Don't trim any of the edges of the jacket, even if you get uneven layering or puckering. The unevenness will be averaged out when you start putting the seams together. Let's assume you're working with a pattern like the ones I use, with shoulder seams that begin at the right and left sides of the neck and go all the way to the wrist. Take the right-front pattern piece and pin it so that it overlaps the edge of the back pattern piece about ½ in. Pin the pieces together and then sew them together with a single straight seam going from one end to the other.

Before you do the other shoulder seam, cut a strip of contrasting, prewashed fabric that's a few inches longer than your seam and about ¾ in. wide. Sew this strip with a single line of straight stitch on top of the lapped seam on the side of the jacket you'll usually wear inside, then go back and do a manual zigzag across the strip to seal the seam, as I'm doing in the right-hand photo on the facing page. Turn the jacket over, change your thread, and cover the seam on the other side with an overlapping line of 2-in. squares. This cre-

Ross's patch pockets are reachable from both sides, because there's a slit at the pocket mouth, so you can get to the patch when it's worn on the inside. This partially completed pocket shows how the slit is finished and the pocket is attached with quilted squares. There's a finished pocket on the jacket shown on the facing page.

Making reversible pockets

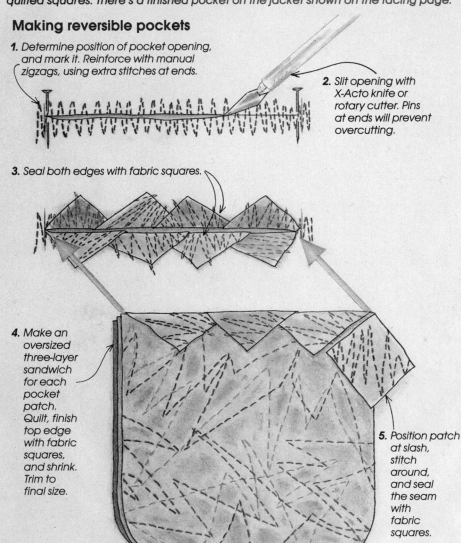

1. Determine position of pocket opening, and mark it. Reinforce with manual zigzags, using extra stitches at ends.

2. Slit opening with X-Acto knife or rotary cutter. Pins at ends will prevent overcutting.

3. Seal both edges with fabric squares.

4. Make an oversized three-layer sandwich for each pocket patch. Quilt, finish top edge with fabric squares, and shrink. Trim to final size.

5. Position patch at slash, stitch around, and seal the seam with fabric squares.

Illustration by Phoebe Gaughan

ates a diamond pattern from the neck to the wrist if you choose a contrast fabric, but it can be almost invisible if you use squares of the same fabric. Either way, cover the squares with more manual zigzag stitch, choosing new thread colors if you like. You are working with a total of eight layers of fabric here, so proceed cautiously. I recommend changing to a new or larger needle.

Once you've completed both shoulder seams, but before you tackle the underarm seam, it's time to finish the edges around the neck, down the front, and across the hem. This will be exactly like finishing the edges on your sample squares and circles. For the really tight curves around the neck, I sometimes use smaller squares because they're easier to shape. Then trim the sleeve ends even, but leave them a little long because they could still shrink a bit, and finish them with the 2-in. squares. For the last time before the jacket is complete, put it in the washer and dryer, then press it thoroughly before you sew the closing seams.

The underarm seams are very straightforward; they're the most like normal sewing of all the steps, because I use a regular right-sides-together seam, and bind it in the usual way. Sew the entire seam, then trim it to ¼ in. Cut two bias strips of contrast fabric 1½ in. wide and the length of one seam plus 2 in. With about 1 in. hanging off at each end, sew one strip right side down on top of the existing seamline with its edge aligned with the trimmed seam allowances. Backstitch at the ends of the seam, then fold the extra lengths back over the seam and turn the strip over the raw edges. You can fold the strip lengthwise to finish its edge, or leave it to be trimmed later; since it's bias, it won't ravel. Then catch it in place by stitching in the ditch next to the first seam.

Making pockets—If you decide to add patch pockets, they will be your last step. Try the jacket on in front of a mirror and check the placement visually. I don't recommend putting the pockets in the side seams because they're harder to get to, and they're not as interesting to look at. The patch pockets (see photo and drawing at left) are completely usable from both sides of the jacket, although the patch is only visible from one side. ☐

Bird Ross lives and maintains her studio in Madison, WI, where she is closing in on her MFA degree in sculpture. She exhibits her work internationally and was featured in the International Textile Competition in Japan this spring.

Whether you go bold or subtle, Ross's quick techniques for machine quilting reversible garments is a great way to explore wearable combinations of color and pattern.

Great Bags from Scraps
Making the most of your leftover fabrics

by Suzen Hahn

i started designing accessories by accident. My hats and bags (like the ones shown at right) grew out of a need to make extra space in my crowded studio. Instead of letting things pile up, I turn my leftover fabric, scraps, and buttons into useful items that cost almost nothing.

The reversible hat can be made in 20 minutes. Cut two 8½-in.-diameter circles for the tops and two rectangles 11 in. wide by 25½ in. long for the brims. Sew each seam with ½-in. allowances, then overcast, press the seam to one side, and topstitch. Stitch the short ends of a brim; repeat for second brim. Clip the seam allowances of each top and one long edge of each brim in quarters. Right sides together, sew a top to each brim, matching the clips, pinning, and easing to fit. Sew the two hats right sides together around the lower edge, leaving an opening. Turn and topstitch the outer edge. Sew four buttons evenly spaced around the sides, and one on top. That's it!

To design a bag for yourself, think about what you will use it for, how much you are willing to haul around, and what style you are most comfortable carrying. One of my company's most popular styles is a knapsack (see the drawings on the facing page for the sewing instructions).

Pulling out your scraps and collected fabrics to make a bag can be an eye-opening experience. You may be surprised to find a common thread in your

Photo by Susan Kahn

collecting. When selecting fabrics, bring a group of possibilities together and then play with what looks good next to what, thinking about how much pattern you want in the bag. Cotton is the most practical, washable, and durable fabric to use for an everyday bag. We also use some rayon fabrics, but they need to be fairly stable in construction and backed with something sturdy, or used in small pieces like pockets or ties.

Compose your bag by cutting out one piece at a time, starting with the largest pieces first. Lay them out on a table in the shape they will have when they are sewn, and then lay down the other pieces, giving you a mock-up of the finished bag. Working this way is similar to collaging; you can see where you need more color or less pattern, and you can experiment with enough variations until it looks good to your eye.

You may find that combining many fabrics in a bag or hat will inspire you to mix and wear clothes in a more interesting way. □

Suzen Hahn is a clothing designer based in Chicago, IL. Her article about her clothing, sold in stores across the country under the name Su-Zen, appeared in Threads *No. 36.*

The easy-to-make hat and bag at left mix five or six different fabrics; every pocket, edging, loop, facing, strap, casing, and lining offers the possibility of additional color and pattern combinations.

Constructing a knapsack

The backpack has two layers: decorative details are sewn to the outer layer, while the inside is a simple lining. Dimensions shown include ½-in. seam allowances throughout.

■ Cut one: pocket, pocket facing, loop strip, casing.
○ Cut two: front, back, flap, strap, strap tie, strap holder.

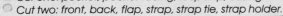

1. Fold and sew loop strip; cut into four pieces.

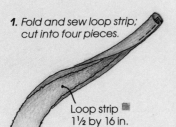

Loop strip ■
1½ by 16 in.

2. Cut two straps 5½ by 14½ in.

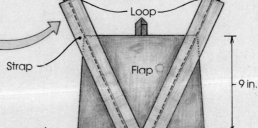

• Cut batting 13½ by 2 in. Center on strap.

• Wrap fabric around batting; pin.

• Insert a loop; stitch end and center.

3. Insert loop between flap and lining, RS together. Stitch along sides and loop edge of flap; turn. Pin straps to raw flap edge as shown.

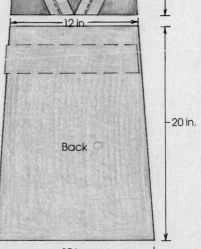

10½ in.

Loop

Strap

Flap

9 in.

4. Fold each tie in half lengthwise, WS out. Stitch side and one end; turn. Topstitch sides.

Strap tie ○
3 by 21 in.

Strap holder 5 in. each side ○

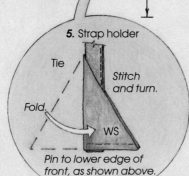

5. Strap holder

Tie

Stitch and turn.

Fold

WS

Pin to lower edge of front, as shown above.

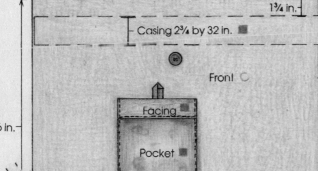

27 in.

1¾ in.

Casing 2¾ by 32 in. ■

Front ○

Facing ■

Pocket ■

26 in.

12 in.

20 in.

Back ○

15 in.

6 in.

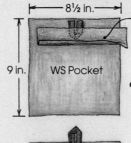

8½ in.

WS Facing

2 in.

9 in.

WS Pocket

RS Pocket

6. Facing decorates the pocket.

• Sew facing to pocket.

• Turn facing to RS pocket and stitch near edge.

• Press pocket edges under. Stitch to RS of front, off center.

7. Stitch lower corners of front (and lining).

8. Sew back to front on lower three sides. (Repeat for lining).

9. Pin back and flap RS together. WS out, slip lining over bag. Sew top edge, leaving a 5-in. opening. Turn and topstitch.

10. Sew short ends of casing. Turn long edges under and press. Stitch around bag, leaving an opening to insert 24-in.-long piece of 1-in.-wide elastic.

11. Add two 1⅛-in. buttons. Tie straps to strap ties with slip knots.

Photo by Susan Kahn

An Intricate Quilt from Simple Blocks

The trick is to plan your pattern for printing rather than piecing

It took only one printing screen to make the blocks for the quilt above. The multiple colors in Karen Soma's "Light and Leaf" quilt (57½ by 40½ in., 1991) come from printing with several transparent dyes.

by Karen Soma

     From *Threads* magazine (March 1993) 45:58-61

most quilters stitch pieces of colored or patterned fabric together to make a block, then repeat the block through a quilt for an overall composition. I simplify the process: I print entire blocks on plain fabric with silkscreens and fabric dyes, then sew the blocks together. The silkscreening process is straightforward (see instructions on p. 70), and an intriguing quilt is possible by creating only one or two motifs to arrange across the surface. The fascinating part is deciding on the motifs and their positioning to create pattern. For me, pattern is a metaphor for life's energy, vibrating and bristling with possibilities. Repeated elements are everywhere, both in the natural and man-made worlds. Here's how I proceed from one motif to a block of four and then arrange the blocks to make a quilt.

Designing a motif

A motif is basically a drawing, such as the top example at right. It can be loose or controlled, simple or complex, depending on your mood. Most of my motifs originate from doodlings. Pencil, pen, felt marker, brush and ink—you can draw with anything that makes a mark. For ease in creating pattern, I choose to make the motif square. Your motif becomes the basic unit of design, repeated to form a pattern.

Experimenting with motif blocks

Once you have some ideas on paper, see how they look repeated. Now the fun really begins! You could draw the paper motif many times, but for faster and more accurate results, use a photocopier. Make at least eight copies of your motif (I make dozens), cut them out, and group them in various configurations. I usually place the motifs in groups of four to see how the edges line up on two different sides (see blocks A and B at right).

Pattern and variations

When you have a few groups of four motifs that you like, paste them down and make several photocopies of each group. Cut them out, then arrange the blocks to get a sense of how the pattern works over a greater expanse. I often alternate these motif blocks in a piece to add variety (see the example directly at right). You can use motifs in a wide range of sizes; I find that the larger the motif size, the more difficult it is to make an interesting composition.

However, a large block doesn't have to stay that way. You can cut it apart into strips, rectangles, or triangles, to intersperse with other colors. This increases

Repeating a Motif

When you rotate and arrange a simple drawn motif in groups of four, you create a new design, as in blocks A and B, at center. The effect becomes even more interesting when the two blocks alternate and repeat over a larger area, as in the pattern at bottom.

Motif

Block A

Block B

color and pattern flow options. Just remember that ¼-in. seams will eat up some of the block size. For example, a 9-in. square cut into eight triangles will, when sewn together, yield a 7-in. square.

Creating diversity

Many factors can alter the look of a basic motif. Color is one of the most obvious. One advantage of printing motifs yourself is that you can rotate the screen and print over the first layer of color with a second color, which gives a more complex design, as in the photo below right. These images were printed with a transparent fabric dye, which also results in a third color where the printings overlap. Printing with an opaque pigment would have a different effect, with the top layer of color covering the image underneath. For more information on dyes and pigments, see "Printing the fabric" on the facing page.

Another way to vary color is to print on different colors of fabric. Yellow printed over white looks quite different from the same yellow printed over pale blue.

For a large motif, such as 9 in., I use a single motif for the screen image. If I want a small motif, I often use blocks of four motifs to make the screen to save assembly time. I may make several screens of variations for one quilt. These related images can be used in a variety of combinations, and can work well when printed over one another.

Assembling the parts

When your fabric is printed and the motifs cut out, it's time to arrange the components, allowing the patterns and colors to work together. This is my favorite part of the process. After you stitch the blocks together, the last design decision is how to quilt the overall composition. Quilting is not just the anchoring of the top, batting, and back, but a final opportunity to add visual interest. An extra shot of color, a line that enhances the shape and rhythm it crosses, can add richness, counterpoint, and emphasis.

Walking a busy city street, dancing to ethnic music, hiking in a windy autumn woods, studying the visual traditions of other times and places, all offer opportunities to experience pattern. Its force and presence surrounds us, its inspiration is everywhere. For me, pattern offers a lifetime of challenge in trying to capture its mystery and magic. □

Karen Soma, a former art teacher, maintains a fiber studio in Seattle, WA, and is currently the president of the Contemporary Quilt Association.

Screen printing

Several methods for making silkscreens exist. I use the photographic emulsion method because it offers a great range of images and detail, and requires a minimum of equipment. Here's how it works: you lay the design, photocopied onto clear acetate, on a screen covered with a light-sensitive coating; expose the screen to light, which hardens the exposed emulsion; and rinse away the balance of the emulsion with water, leaving the image of your design on the screen. Paint spread on the screen prints only in the uncovered areas.

Preparing a design—Once you've decided on the final design, draw it precisely with a permanent black felt marker on white paper, making it dark. Precision counts: If lines at edges must match, check them for alignment now. Even a 1mm mistake in the width or length of a screen image can, when repeated across an entire quilt, result in ill-fitting patterns and lopsided shapes and borders.

Be careful to eliminate all stray marks, which will reproduce as part of the design. Then have the image photocopied onto two sheets of clear acetate at a print shop. You'll stack the sheets together so the image is totally dark, and tape them together at the edges on two sides to prevent shifting.

The photographic emulsion method—The Speedball Screen Printing Instruction booklet, available free from Hunt Manufacturing Co. (Customer Service Dept., PO Box 5819, Statesville, NC 28687-5819) provides detailed instructions for the photographic emulsion method. You'll need a screen prepared with a light-sensitive coating, a light source to

Overprinting a silkscreen design with other transparent colors offers design variations. The upper left square, screenprinted just once in rust, is the basic design. The other three squares are overprinted with the same screen rotated three different ways using a total of three colors.

Screen printing in progress: author Karen Soma, shown above, pulls paint across the screen with a squeegee (left). The pencil lines on the fabric guide screen placement. The photocopied (black and clear) acetate sheet helps in visualizing the effect of overprinting. Note the printed areas in blue and green.

transfer the opaque image from the acetate to the coated screen, and a piece of dull-edged glass that fits inside the frame. You can buy screens ready made, or frames and fabric to make your own, at art supply stores.

For a light-sensitive coating, I use the Speedball Bichromate System, which involves mixing four parts emulsion to one part sensitizer. Working over a sink, pour some solution (two or three teaspoons for a 12- by 18-in. screen) on the prepared screen; spread evenly with a squeegee. Repeat on the other side. Dry the screen away from heat or light (such as in a dark cupboard or closet). Once it's dry, keep the screen in the closet until you're ready to expose it.

You'll need to prepare a light source. I use a 250 watt photoflood bulb from a photo supply store, set in a disposable aluminum-foil pie pan as a reflector. The Speedball instructions recommend a distance from light to screen and exposure times.

To prepare the exposure area, lay a piece of black paper as large as the screen on a table. Working quickly, place the screen flat side down on the paper. Lay the acetate positives, then the glass, on top of the screen. The glass provides even, close contact with the screen, vital for retaining fine details. Expose the screen for the required time.

After exposure, apply a forceful stream of tepid water to wash both sides of the screen. I suggest working away from food-preparation areas; a sprayer or aerated faucet on the bathtub works well. The water washes the emulsion from the unexposed areas, where the dark area of your motif blocked the light. Your design will look clear and the surrounding area opaque. You can *gently* scrub the mesh with a short bristle brush; too much scrubbing can destroy the details. Let the screen dry thoroughly, then use a water-resistant tape, such as duct tape, to cover both sides of the frame plus the mesh area not taken up by the design.

Printing the fabric—I print on 100 percent cotton fabric, washed to remove all sizing. If I want a different background color, I often dye the fabric with a fiber-reactive dye before printing. You'll need to stretch and tape the fabric until smooth, but not taut, over a large flat surface; a plywood sheet covered with foam-backed vinyl makes a good printing table. Draw a pencil grid on the fabric with squares slightly larger than the design, leaving at least ½ in. around each image for seam allowances. The pencil lines should extend from edge to edge of the fabric, so even though the frame is much larger than the actual image, you can use the ends of the lines as guides.

My favorite fabric dye is liquid Procion H, available by mail from Cerulean Blue (PO Box 21168, Seattle, WA 98111-3168; 800-676-8602; free catalog). If you want to print a light color on a darker background, however, use opaque fabric pigments. I like a pigment called Unidye, which can be ordered from Union (453 Broad Ave., Ridgefield, NJ 07657; 800-526-0455; free catalog). It's easy to set and it leaves the fabric softer after washing than many other brands of pigment do.

I print in every other space, let the dye dry for a couple of hours, and then print the skipped spaces (otherwise the screen would contact wet dye and cause smearing). After the second printing dries, you can begin overprinting, or printing the same fabric a second time. The acetate transparencies come in handy now. If you lay a transparency down on a print, you can see the effect that overprinting will have (see the left-hand photo above). Rotate to discover new images.

I print considerably more fabric than I will need so that I have plenty of choices when I begin arranging the blocks. The leftovers often find their way into other quilts.

After completing all the printing, set the colors permanently, as instructed by the dye or pigment manufacturer, and the fabric is ready to use. —K.S.

Quilt Meets Soft Toy

Padding and stitching add structure with less batting

by Judith Duffey

Quilting gives this menagerie of soft toys both their playful personalities and their structure. The easy one-piece bat hangs from a branch via hook-and-loop tape ovals sewn on his legs. The chameleon has a childproof padded eye, a multicolored convertible coat, and a curvy thread-gathered tail. Scales projecting from the dinosaur's back create an illusion of bulk; without them he's really just a curved piece of padded fabric. Removing the hood of the soft quilted car converts it to a sturdy wagon. The axles are zigzagged rods of fabric.

Q: When is a quilt not a quilt?

A: When it is a color-changing chameleon, a wagon that converts to a car, a flapping bat, or a spiky dinosaur.

Using quilting to design and make soft toys brings distinct advantages over traditional stuffed toys. Quilted toys depend on the stiffness of quilted layers for much of their shape, reducing the messy job of stuffing. Padded, stitched shapes can be stacked, folded, coiled, stretched, or joined at the edges to create three-dimensional shapes. With less filling, the toys are easily washable, quick to dry, and will pack flat for travel.

If you've wanted to try quilting but find a bed quilt a daunting prospect, try these smaller, relatively quick projects. For both novice and experienced quilters, applying the technique to toys keeps all the pleasure of intricate color piecing and the interplay of light and shadow as the stitched designs emerge. And it combines the tactile delight of the quilting process with speedy and satisfying results.

The motley tribe of unusual creatures shown on the facing page came about as a result of the marriage of two obsessions: quilts and toys. My sister Phyllis Ford and I combined interests as diverse as quilting, sculpture, natural history, art therapy, and teaching to develop toys that are really little three-dimensional quilts; they rely on padded, stitched fabric forms for stability and structure.

In developing these toys, we were carrying on a family tradition of quilting. The project also placed us within the quilting tradition in another way. Because the toys evolved mainly over a difficult summer spent in hospital waiting rooms, they linked us to the pioneer quilters who used their quilting to cope with chaotic lives and trying circumstances.

Design approaches

Our very different backgrounds led us to two distinct approaches. Phyllis' study of biology leads her to approach toy design from the observation of animals' natural skin or body structures. She finds photographs in library books or magazines like *The National Geographic* that show "natural" quilts—the hexagons of a turtle shell, or the elaborately patterned furrows of a rhino's hide. A bat's wing folds along lines that are both decorative and aerodynamically functional. Then she translates the natural structures into three-dimensional ones that can be built from flat shapes. Some structures, like the curve of the chameleon's legs and tail, call for new techniques in handling fabric, which I describe under "Special effects" on p. 74. These new techniques in turn spark off other links between natural and constructed forms.

My own approach is to develop toys by playing with shapes to see what they would like to be. The connection with an animal might come later. Playing with a piece of pita bread led to several toys. I noticed that a pita cut in half forms a semicircle, open at one end. It can be a container, and when opened, the flat edge forms a base that allows the structure to stand. By translating the shape into two joined quilted semicircles, different toys emerge with the addition of wings, feet, or feathers. Using this "pita principle," playing with my food led to a set of nested chickens, a car body, and a frog mask that reverses to become a prince.

Other kinds of manipulation of quilted shapes, such as origami folding, coiling, and stacking, allow a flat padded piece of fabric to become an owl, a car wheel, or a stable foot for a bird marionette.

Working together, my sister and I began to adapt elements of the other's approach. A quilting structure originally seen in a real creature might be the starting point for an imaginary one, or an invented structure could suggest new similarities to natural forms. Combining the two design approaches generated a whole new series of ideas and made us think about the design process in a more flexible way.

Developing your own patterns

Decide which design approach fits you best and come up with some toy ideas of your own. Here are some suggestions:

First choose your starting point. It may be mainly visual, like an armadillo's patchwork coat, or mostly structural, like the way a grasshopper's leg folds. The fastening structures of ordinary sewing offer many starting points: a separable zipper and buttons turn a flat tail into a cape; belt loops hold up long floppy ears; an old-fashioned garter becomes the nose of a grumpy witch. Reversible pockets hide endless possibilities for changing personalities. Besides lending unique character traits, these fastenings lead to inventive teaching toys.

If you're working from the animal to the toy, your source material will be important. Get good photos from different angles. Analyze the forms, breaking complex shapes down into cylinders, boxes, or hemispheres. Don't be afraid to simplify. To make sure you understand how the shapes fit together, it may help to make a clay model. Then think of making shells or solids for the different parts. Use roughly quilted scrap fabrics as working material for your rough draft. Translate these into quilted 3-D shapes by pinning the flat shapes around the model.

Don't worry about being too realistic. Decide what the most unusual (or quilt-like) features are—(the long, curvy neck; the puckered mouth; the ridged tail?)—and emphasize them. When you are satisfied with your assembly of shapes, record them on paper. This is your pattern.

If you decide to work the opposite way, by playing with shapes and fastenings to see what kind of creature they suggest, start by making a few different flat padded shapes. Then try different ways of putting them together. Turn, twist, fold, and change them the way young children play with objects, investigating every possibility without thinking too much. Suddenly the way a shape changes will remind you of an object or a personality, and you're nearly there. Add whatever details—ears, eyes, wings, feet—seem necessary. Then record your exact shapes and procedures. Don't be afraid to keep the structures and details simple, and don't worry if the creature is unlike any you've ever seen. Less realistic detail leaves more room for imaginative play.

Basic construction

Toys can be any size; our largest model is about 12 in. long and requires less than ¾ yard of fabric. Lightweight, tightly woven cottons work best, because they're easy to turn in a narrow space and less likely to fray around ears and toes. Loosely woven fabrics like velvet or corduroy can be useful for special textural effects. Strengthen them with lightweight iron-on interfacing to help prevent fraying.

The dinosaur shown in the photo on the facing page and in the drawing on p. 74 illustrates several techniques we've used for our quilted toys. The basic principle of construction is to assemble separate padded shapes: First, place fabric and facing right sides together on top of a layer of batting. For small pieces like feet, mark and stitch the seams through all layers before cutting the shapes. You can omit the marking by stitching around a template of the pattern pinned or taped to the fabric. Be sure to leave an opening for turning (see the drawing on p. 74). Then cut out pieces, leaving a narrow seam allowance. Trim, clip curves and corners, and turn, easing out points and small shapes from the inside. Slip-stitch the opening closed by hand.

Next, quilt the individual padded pieces by hand or machine. The quilting provides the shape with stability and body. You could quilt in concentric lines that echo the shape of the piece or just

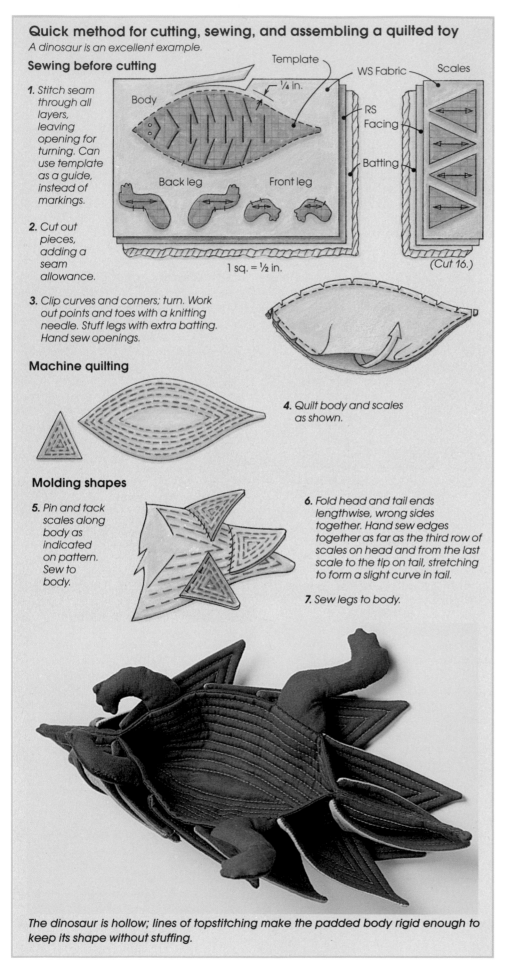

Quick method for cutting, sewing, and assembling a quilted toy

A dinosaur is an excellent example.

Sewing before cutting

1. Stitch seam through all layers, leaving opening for turning. Can use template as a guide, instead of markings.

2. Cut out pieces, adding a seam allowance.

3. Clip curves and corners; turn. Work out points and toes with a knitting needle. Stuff legs with extra batting. Hand sew openings.

Machine quilting

4. Quilt body and scales as shown.

Molding shapes

5. Pin and tack scales along body as indicated on pattern. Sew to body.

6. Fold head and tail ends lengthwise, wrong sides together. Hand sew edges together as far as the third row of scales on head and from the last scale to the tip on tail, stretching to form a slight curve in tail.

7. Sew legs to body.

Template
WS Fabric
Scales
Body
¼ in.
RS
Facing
Batting
Back leg *Front leg*
1 sq. = ½ in.
(Cut 16.)

The dinosaur is hollow; lines of topstitching make the padded body rigid enough to keep its shape without stuffing.

quilt randomly over the whole surface. Match or contrast the thread to the fabric for different effects. You may decide to match the fabric on one side of the padded piece and contrast on the other, match both sides (with different colors in the needle and bobbin), or use contrasting thread on both sides. Avoid pressing the fabric after the batting has been added; pressing will flatten the batting and obscure the quilting lines.

Finally, assemble the padded, quilted shapes according to the pattern that you've developed.

Special effects

You will quickly find your own uses for the special techniques we developed for our toys. By manipulating padded shapes as you feed them through the sewing machine, you build in curves and waves. (See drawings A and B on the facing page.) Take care not to pull the needle off center; it can damage the machine and/or break the needle.

Topstitching provides most of the details for a simple one-piece toy like the bat. Stitching defines his body, legs, and wing folds, We added extra batting to the body for a rounder shape. (See the photo on p. 72).

Use a template to machine embroider details before padding. For the chameleon's mouth, we cut a template for the lower jaw, taped it to the fabric, and satin-stitched the mouth along the upper template edge. (See the photo on p. 72.)

You can create solids by alternately topstitching and folding a padded piece, or by coiling strips of bias-cut padded fabric. (See drawings C and D on the facing page). Or you can create the illusion of a solid by sewing a series of quilted forms to project away from a flat base, like the scales on the dinosaur's back. This technique results in a visually solid form the same way that a row of dominoes suggests a solid wall.

The chameleon's padded eye is safe for young children (no buttons to chew off and swallow). Its stuffed tail is formed by a series of gathered areas tightened into a beaded curl, echoing the curving layers of its bright coat. (See these features in the photo on p. 72 and in drawings E, F, and G on the facing page.)

Use our techniques (and the chameleon's flexibility) as starting points for your own family of quilted toys. New problems will generate new solutions and lead to your own growing vocabulary of forms and special effects. □

Judith Duffey is an art historian and fiber artist living and working in London.

Special effects for shaping your own quilted pieces

Add dimension to flat shapes by manipulating fabric feed. Create solids by coiling, folding, and padding. Make a 3-D curve with gathering and coiling. Layer a multicolored coat.

Adding dimension

A. Curves—Lifting fabric while topstitching a foot stretches bottom surface more than top. Stitching locks curve in place. Flip second foot of a pair so both feet curve into the body.

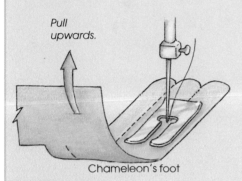

Pull upwards.

Chameleon's foot

B. Waves—Cut a shape from padded fabric. Stretch it gently toward you as you zigzag raw edge. Stretching creates a curvy edge for ears, feathers, and other details.

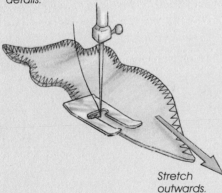

Stretch outwards.

Creating solids

C. Solid rod—Zigzag heavily on rectangular padded piece. Fold and zigzag through all layers; repeat. If piece won't fit under presser foot, sew final edges by hand. For round car axle, roll finished piece between fingers.

Continue to fold in half and zigzag through all layers.

D. Coiling—Cut fabric, facing, and batting in long bias strips as for dinosaur pieces, p. 74. Stitch, leaving one end open. Turn; stitch lengthwise through all layers. To form wheel, sew closed end to one end of axle. Firmly roll strip, anchoring with a few hand stitches to prevent shift.

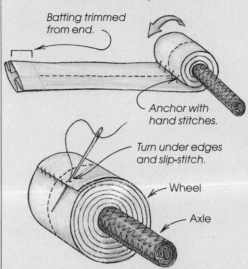

Batting trimmed from end.

Anchor with hand stitches.

Turn under edges and slip-stitch.

Wheel

Axle

E. Padded eye—Trace eye circle on fabric; cut out, adding seam allowance. Place on backing fabric, and stitch ¾ of the way around circle. Stuff with batting, complete stitching, and trim to shape. On head piece, divide eye circle into eight equal sections; clip lines from center to edge of circle. Fold sections to WS; press. Center eyehole over padded eye piece and baste. Topstitch around eyehole.

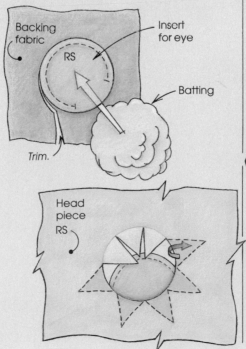

Backing fabric

RS

Insert for eye

Batting

Trim.

Head piece RS

3-D curves and layers

F. A curvy tail—Insert needle (with knotted thread) into tip of tail and emerge on underside ½ in. away. Sew a ring of running stitches and pull tightly to gather. Secure with a stitch. Insert needle again, emerging ¾ in. away. Repeat process for entire tail.

Gradually increase distance between rings.

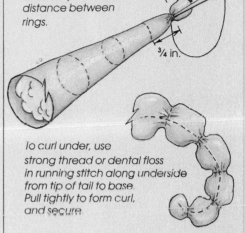

½ in.

¾ in.

To curl under, use strong thread or dental floss in running stitch along underside from tip of tail to base. Pull tightly to form curl, and secure.

G. Color changing layers—Cut a pair of coat shapes in each color. Right sides together, match shapes of adjacent colors (for example, red/purple). Stitch outside edge of each pair; clip, turn, and topstitch. To assemble, match right sides of identical colors and stitch open edge. For last seam, turn in seam allowances and hand sew. Topstitch each "page" close to central seam. Sew to toy.

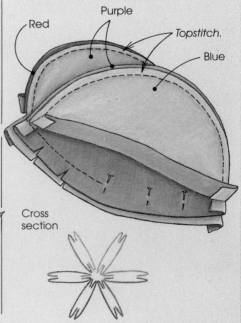

Red

Purple

Topstitch.

Blue

Cross section

Illustrations by Jean Galli

Kids and Quilts

Appliqué with colorful felt is an easy skill to master

by Judy Langille

uiltmaking and children go together like ice cream and hot fudge. My young art students always love the quilts we make together—from the sewing or painting to the snuggly warmth and texture of the finished quilt.

Each child in the class designs and makes at least one square. Very young children can use fabric markers or paint, while the eight- or nine-year-olds appliqué felt and embroider. Themes that children are most interested in work best. They range from self-portraits to class subjects such as the alphabet, animals, insects, and fairy tales. I think it's important that the children be involved in the whole quiltmaking process so that they learn about quilting, in addition to sewing and painting. Besides, they take tremendous pride in their accomplishment when the quilt *they've made* is finally hung.

Making a square

Each square starts as a sketch by a child. If the drawing is too small, it can be photocopied to enlarge it to size. The sketch

A whole class of elementary school students comes to life in "Junior II." The children drew their pictures first and then sewed appropriately colored felt to a backing square. Yarn hair and embroidered names complete the squares, and quilt assembly is a group project.

From *Threads* magazine (July 1993) 47:42-43

A science unit on insects can prompt a quilt. For this one, children captured and drew each bug before rendering it in felt.

serves as a guide as well as a tracing foundation for pattern pieces. The children use fabric scissors to cut out their pieces from a large assortment of colored felt, which is easy to cut and sew.

Next, the children learn to appliqué by first pinning and then sewing the large pieces to the background square with a double strand of embroidery floss and a small running stitch. I've found that the extra length and large eye of a No. 18 chenille needle (available from The Cotton Patch, 1025 Brown Ave., Lafayette, CA 94549; 800-835-4418) is most comfortable for young sewers. After sewing on the large shapes, the kids add the secondary ones.

Children love to stuff the parts of their design that should protrude—like noses—with batting. And their creativity simply blossoms when they're presented with plenty of embellishment materials such as beads, sequins, ribbons, rickrack, yarn, and feathers. Another skill the children enjoy learning is how to use simple embroidery stitches such as chain and stem stitch to draw details and to sign their names or label the block's subject.

Designing the quilt top

Probably the most fun of all for a group of kids is deciding how to arrange the squares for the best looking quilt (they also learn a lot about cooperation and compromise without realizing it). If the children are old enough and can sew well enough, they'll have fun using a running stitch to frame their own squares with borders. Otherwise, you'll have to do it. Next, if possible, help them take turns sewing the squares into strips and joining the strips to form the whole top on the sewing machine. You'll need to supervise the use of the machine carefully, but older kids will quickly learn how to use it safely.

Layering and finishing the quilt

To prevent shifting and wrinkling, have the children tape the backing fabric (muslin is fine) to the floor, right side down. It should be at least 4 in. larger on all sides than the quilt top so they can also bind the quilt's edges with it. Next they will smooth a medium-loft batting over the backing and place the top, right side up, on top.

Hand quilting is much too tedious for children, so we always tie our quilts in the borders with cotton crochet thread or polyester yarn. Kids love pushing their needle through all three layers of the quilt until it touches the floor before bringing it up. Then everyone learns to tie a square knot, something many adults have trouble doing: right over left, then left over right.

Binding is the last step. To avoid the complexities of a separate bias strip, fold the edges of the backing fabric onto the top. Either you or the kids should pin it in place. Then turn under a seam allowance to make a neat edge, and pin it. Since it's important that the binding be secured firmly, I always encourage the children to sew it to the top with a visible overcast stitch, using crochet cotton or sewing thread. Finally, we attach a 3-in.-wide sleeve to the back for a hanging rod, and choose a prominent space in the school to hang our quilt. □

Judy Langille of Lawrenceville, NJ, is an elementary school art teacher and an avid quilter.

Fabric and Floss in Relief

Stitches and stuffing turn textiles into pictures and pins

by Salley Mavor

For the leopards in "Rana Is Born" (20 by 18 by 1½ in.), author Salley Mavor dyed velveteen fabric yellow speckled with brown and embroidered the black spots. She used an antique brocade for the background in the upper right, reinforcing the tears with embroidery stitches. The techniques used to make the three-dimensional animals can also be used to create pins. (Photo by Susan Kahn)

From *Threads* magazine (July 1992) 41:48-50

started sewing bits and pieces of fabric together with beads, buttons, and snaps when I was a small child. And I'm doing it again today, making fabric relief "paintings" of stuffed and embroidered textile forms. I rediscovered my original creative medium in art school. Experimenting with different mixed media, I found that a good way to hold materials together was to sew and bind them with thread. It was easy to change things around and undo what I didn't like by cutting the thread.

All my compositions are sewn by hand, even the satin-stitched border lines that frame many of my works including "Rana Is Born," shown on the facing page. I like a little calculated imperfection in a picture and find machine stitching too regular and even. Hand stitching over and over around the edge of fabric intensifies the quality and softness of a picture. There is something so sure about this medium, unlike paint. Embroidery floss has no fuzzy edges, you can put one fabric against another but each remains distinct, and I make fewer mistakes because of the slow pace of the sewing. It takes the time it takes to come out right, no more, no less.

I often work out the basic design and shape of a picture in my notebook, then let the details develop over time as I make trees and foliage. I use new as well as antique fabrics, often dyeing purchased fabric to achieve the look I want. I embellish the reliefs with embroidery, beads, buttons, and silk leaves. You can try out these techniques on a small scale by making a pin, as I explain later on.

Three-dimensional forms

I make the stuffed, three-dimensional shapes of animals, trees, and so forth as separate forms that I can rearrange until I decide on their location. Only the fronts, which will show, have to look good. The backs of the shapes are crossed by a maze of messy stitches that will never show, as you can see from the back of the elephant in the photo on p. 80. I make sure the pieces are sewn together securely enough to be manipulated and handled by family members, guests, and sometimes pets.

For the leopards in "Rana Is Born," I cut out cardboard shapes of the bodies, heads, and legs separately. I covered the cardboard shapes with fabric and then stuffed the shapes with fiberfill to make them puffy and more three-dimensional. When it came time to assemble the pieces, I positioned the limbs and sewed them to the body.

Dyeing

I covered the leopards in "Rana Is Born" with velveteen fabric that I dyed yellow with brown spots using cold-water Procion MX dyes. I considered dyeing black spots onto the yellow and brown, but decided instead to embroider all the black spots. I need a lot of time to think about what I'm doing, and embroidery forces me to slow down. When working with a wet, flowing medium like dye, I tend to speed up and jump around, spraying and painting large pieces of fabric. Dyeing fabric is a fun contrast to the sedate, intricate stitching, but it doesn't work for me to dye something that I want to have control over.

Sometimes I paint Procion on the fabric with a paintbrush, but mostly I like the spatter effect achieved by spraying layers of small dots and splotches. I use an ordinary plant mister to spray the dye (I work outside). This is a crude form of airbrushing which I find spontaneous and surprising in its results. The random pattern created has subtle variations of color and texture that come close to nature.

The manufacturer of Procion suggests that for best results you use new, nonsynthetic fabrics that have no sizing; these can be purchased through mail order. But if you want to use an old or a used fabric, dye a sample to see if the dye will take to the fabric. I once dyed the worn, blue fabric from an old pair of pants because I

liked the texture and weave and could not find anything similar in the fabric store. It worked fine, and I achieved the results I wanted. There is room for experimentation with many different fabrics.

Antique fabrics

Old fabrics such as worn brocade or upholstery fabric have wonderful color variations. There is history in a fabric that has been sat upon for a number of years. Such fabrics bring a unique spirit and quality to a piece of artwork. Of course antique cloth tends to rip and fall apart easily and needs extra care and attention. When I use an old or antique fabric, I try to overlap it on a stronger fabric. I reinforce the old, fragile areas with many small running stitches, repairing any rips that develop through handling. I try to make the reinforcement stitches decorative by having them conform to shapes around them. I used an ancient brocade for background areas of "Rana Is Born" (you can see it, and the reinforcing of tears in the fabric, behind the trees in the upper right part of the photo). I also used antique fabrics for some of the three-dimensional insects shown in the photo below.

After any dyeing and setting or repair of background fabrics, I cut out pieces of

Insects from antique fabrics, soft sculpture, and embroidery: *For the legs of the beetles and cricket, the author covered twisted wire with grosgrain and satin ribbons. She used parts of hooks and eyes to create the insects' mouths and eyes.*

Making soft-sculpture pins

It's fun and easy to make whimsical brooches using these techniques. A few are shown in the photo below. Cut cardboard for the shapes. Cut fabric for the back and front with ½-in. seam allowances. Stitch the front to the back, right sides together, leaving an opening for inserting the cardboard. Turn right sides out. Insert the cardboard, then stuff the front of the shape with fiberfill. Stitch the opening closed (see the elephant in the photo below). To create shapes that are more three-dimensional, like the insects in the photo on p. 79, use soft-sculpture techniques, with cardboard for stiffness if necessary.

For tree trunks (at top of photo), you can wrap twisted strands of electrical wire with fabric, stitching the fabric together at the back. For stems and small tree branches (left side of photo), wrap florist wire with embroidery floss. You can decorate your pin before and after assembling the shape. Add embroidery, buttons, beads, trim, and so forth. For the seeds of the watermelon pin, for example, I used black seed beads. Stitch a pin back, available at sewing and craft stores, to the back of the pin. — *S.M.*

the fabrics and play around with their positioning, sometimes overlapping layers. I turn under the edges and then hand stitch them in place.

Trees

To make a tree, I start with a couple of lengths of electrical wire and twist them together into a strong, flexible armature for the trunk. I cover the wire with a strip of fabric, sometimes adding fiberfill for a thicker trunk, and sew a back seam. I like fabrics with color variations in the weave, such as wool or fabrics with a woven pattern. I make smaller branches from single strands of fabric-covered wire and sew them to the trunk. I then embellish trunk and branches with embroidery floss of various colors, making French knots and tiny stitches like dots and dashes.

I buy artificial silk flowers and leaves for the trees and plants. I can cut the silk leaves into any shape without them fraying and also color them with permanent felt-tipped markers. I make stems and small tree branches with thin florist or copper beading wire that I wrap with embroidery floss. I find that using a single strand of thread works best, as a double or triple strand tends to get lumpy. I also use a single strand for most of the embroidery, because it gives me a more controlled, delicate, fine line.

Assembly

When I have finished making all the three-dimensional pieces and placed them in their proper locations, I make a simple drawing noting their positions. I draw on the background with a fabric pencil to indicate where the embroidery should go. I then remove all the three-dimensional shapes and embroider the background. Mostly I use just a few embroidery stitches, including seeding stitch, Rumanian stitch, French knots, and a modified version of stem stitch. I do not use an embroidery hoop, because it can damage and stretch the delicately layered background fabric. When the embroidery is finished, I stretch the background fabric onto a wooden stretcher frame. Then, referring to the drawing, I sew the three-dimensional pieces into place, stitching from back to front around their outside edges. I tack the plants into place with a few stitches here and there. I frame my fabric reliefs under glass, in a shallow window-box type frame, to protect them from dust. ☐

Salley Mavor made fabric reliefs to illustrate the children's book The Way Home *by Judith Benét Richardson (Macmillan Pub. Co., 1991).*

A Quilt Style of Your Own

Finding a way through the maze of techniques takes insight and lots of practice

by Erika Carter

be it knitting, needlepoint, crochet, or sewing, I've always enjoyed crafting a product. I love to feel the materials changing in my hands. So, in 1984, when my favorite yarn shop began offering quilting lessons, I thought I'd give them a try. I was first drawn to traditional quilts, but my teacher, Barbara Sorenson, was quilting original wall hangings and clothes. Inspired, I soon realized that quilting was a medium that motivated me to think artistically.

Because I've never been attracted to using traditional artistic media like paint, I'd never thought of myself as an artist, even though my mother is a painter. But seeing Barbara's work convinced me that I'd like to try to make art. It was like discovering I wanted to talk, even though I had no idea yet what I wanted to say. What follows is a description of how I developed a language of my own out of all the possibilities open to quilters today, a language that has enabled me to explore not only the quilter's craft, but also my feelings about my own life and everything I find meaningful. My "language" is technically very simple. The quilts shown here and on pp. 84 and 85 are all examples of it; I've described my process in detail in "Making a strip quilt," on p. 82.

Studying and practicing

Just as a writer can only find his or her style by writing prolifically, I knew I'd have to make a lot of quilts so I took classes for a couple of years, studying various techniques and styles. I had no clear image in mind of what I wanted to do; I just followed my instincts about what was interesting or appealing. First I experimented with block forms, taking ideas and exercises from quilt authors like Michael James and Jeffrey Gutcheon (see "Further reading" on p. 83). I used both solids and prints, embellishing my work

Erika Carter explored virtually every corner of the contemporary quilt world to find her own style, and the technique with which to pursue it. Her machine-pieced, hand-appliquéd quilt "Cottonwoods" (62½ in. by 47 in.; 1991), is a recent example of where her search has led. For a report on her journey, read on; she explains her techniques on p. 82.

From *Threads* magazine (May 1992) 40:39-43

Making a strip quilt

Carter (left) considers her palettes of pre-cut strips of patterned cottons, as she composes a background for one of her images. To create the soft diagonals in her backgrounds, Carter seams the fabric strips together with their ends offset by ¼ in., then trims off the staggered edges (above). All her cutting is done with a rotary cutter and a straightedge.

Occasionally I begin with a sketch of what I might appliqué to a background so I have an idea of how the background color should be composed: where I need high contrast, and where I need to suggest shadows, or something distant. More often than not, however, I simply begin with my fabrics. From my supply, organized and visible on a bookshelf, I choose my palette, arranging my selection in piles from light to dark. If I know that the background will suggest sky, trees, and ground cover, for instance, I might organize three piles, one each of lights, mediums, and darks. I often use 25-50 different fabrics per quilt.

Then, using a rotary cutter, a 6½-in. by 24-in. plastic ruler, and a cutting mat, I cut my fabrics into strips. First, with the fabric folded once, selvages together, I make a crossgrain cut from fold to selvage to create a long 1½-in.-wide strip. I then cut this strip into 6½-in. segments using the width of my ruler as a guide. I don't evaluate the various sections of each print; I just cut as much as I think I'll need into strips and stack them, one stack per fabric.

Next, I arrange the stacks on "palettes." For portability I use large pieces of cardboard, as you can see in the left-hand photo above. With my palettes on a table, I begin arranging the strips, one at a time, in columns and in alternating diagonals, on a large piece of felt hung on the wall. I feel it is very important to work on a vertical surface if that's the way the finished work is to be seen.

When the composition pleases me, I take down in careful order one column of strips at a time, with the top strip in the composition on the top of the pile. I then sew the strips together, offsetting the long seams by ¼ in. to the left or right to create the desired diagonal slant, as in the right-hand photo above. After pressing all seam allowances down, I trim the staggered edges off to get a clean, straight edge, then return the trimmed panel to the wall. After repeating this process for each panel, I sew them together with lengthwise seams, pressing the seam allowances in the same direction.

Upon this background, I then compose whatever appliqué I might add, pinning the strips in place. For my palette I cut long fabric strips and press under the edges to prepare them for appliquéing. I cut the strips to length as I decide I need them, folding in the ends as I complete the appliqué when I'm satisfied with the composition.

I rarely cut away the background from behind the appliqué because I like the stability the background gives the finished wall hanging. But if the appliqué happens to be a large tree trunk, I'll piece this in by machine. After composing the tree trunk on the wall, and sewing its strips together, I trim it to the desired finished width plus ½ in. for two seam allowances. I carefully pin the trunk to the background so it can't shift and move the whole ensemble to a large cutting mat. I cut the background with a rotary cutter and a straightedge ½ in. inside along both edges of the trunk. I slip the straightedge under the trunk, then lift the trunk fabric out of the way. I sew the trunk to the background and iron the ¼-in. seam allowances towards the trunk.

My next step is to square the entire piece. Usually this means trimming only the top and bottom edges of the background and not the sides. Any minor differences in the measurements are corrected when attaching the border, which I compose and sew from strips. I then attach the border, mitering the corners.

After basting the top, batting, and backing together with large stitches along the panel seams and in the border, I hand quilt, without a frame, along the vertical panel lines and around any appliqué, as well as some lines in the border. If I need to mark quilting lines, I use ¼-in.-wide masking tape or a chalk wheel. When the quilt edges are bound, I finish it by embroidering the name, my signature, and the date.

Then I immediately begin another piece! —E.C.

with lots of hand quilting. At the same time, I explored all kinds of fabrics, including lamés and satins, corduroys, and bonded tricot. And I started collecting, and poring over, books about quilt art.

I also joined a local quilt group. I was lucky to have one nearby that focused on art quilts: Seattle's Contemporary Quilt Association. I'm still a member, and the people I've met at the monthly meetings have become an invaluable support group. Right from the start I found it invigorating to have a regular opportunity to see other quilters' work, to hear their ideas, and to meet people working on similar projects. If nothing else, the next meeting has always been a great excuse to finish my current piece. It was support from my fellow quilters that convinced me to start entering quilt shows, which I did whenever I had a piece that I felt strongly about.

Seeing a common element

Within about two years I had produced approximately 25 wall hangings. It was only then that I began to recognize the common element in my work. I was fascinated with texture and color. This realization made it a lot easier to focus my efforts. I had a brainstorming session with a fellow quilter in which we thought of as many ways as possible to introduce texture into our work. I experimented with pleats, folding them back and forth, and with stitched on objects like beads and yarn. I even tried crumpling up and shredding the fabrics I was quilting.

I was impressed with the effect of yarns added to the quilted surface, so I began a deliberate series using strips to which I hand appliquéd cotton and synthetic yarns. Each successive wall hanging explored a new challenge: dark to light in one color range; dark to light with alternating color ranges; using curved strips (I'll never try that again!); and creating an assembled background which was then cut into curved pieces and resewn.

In retrospect, the most important experiences of those early days were a couple of workshops I took with nationally recognized quilters. The first was with Roberta Horton, known for her subtle use of prints, especially in Japanese fabrics. Our project was to design a quilt using a single shape. I chose an elongated triangle, cut out dozens of them in a host of different fabrics, and experienced for the first time the pleasure of composing with precut fabric. Up to now I'd been cutting out new fabrics as I went along, but separating the cutting from the decision making was a revelation, especially when combined with the complete interchangeability of the identical pieces.

I'd often worked with repeated blocks, but here I was creating an overall surface with a single repeated element, any one of which could be replaced with a more appropriate choice for whatever effect I was pursuing. Roberta showed us how she covered a wall with a large piece of white felt to which the fabric would stick, allowing her to compose an entire quilt without making a stitch. I've adopted this idea wholeheartedly, as you can see in the left-hand picture on the facing page.

Some time later I took a workshop with internationally acclaimed quilt artist Nancy Crow. She observed all the effort I was exerting to create texture by appliquéing yarns to fabric strips. It was her suggestion that, rather than concentrating on three-dimensional texture, I try using color to create *visual* texture. This idea excited me. I hadn't considered color as texture before, but it made sense. I must admit, too, that I was relieved to think I could reduce some of the time-consuming hand work and concentrate on design. Seeing Nancy's incredible commitment to her career as a quilt artist was also very inspiring to me. I'll never forget her telling us that there's always something more to say in one's work, and there is always room to grow.

As my decisions about *how* to quilt narrowed to my current technique, I began to uncover *what* it was that I wanted my quilting to accomplish: to help me better communicate my excitement about the world around me, my love of nature, and the importance of a healthy environment.

On my own

I'm now very clear about what I'm trying to do: By appliquéing rectangular strips and squares of fabric to a strip-pieced background, I create abstract, fragmented suggestions of trees and other natural imagery. Through the use of color, I attempt to direct the observer's eye across and around the composition. I create my quilts almost entirely from identically shaped strips of large-scale prints in cotton fabric. These prints, when cut, lose their subject definition and can be used for their color, texture, and pattern.

Because of the manageable dimensions of my 1-in. by 6-in. background fabric strips (I sometimes refer to them as "long strokes"), I can quickly compose and make changes on my felt wall. I sometimes insert small pieces into the strips to add color and visual texture. These "short strokes" can also be used to create contrasting highlights or subtle blends between prints. By placing the strips slightly on the diagonal, the stripped background works to balance the often vertical and horizontal appliquéd lines of my imagery. The diagonals also create a sense of movement (another form of texture) that I can enhance with my choice of color.

I am very much involved in my work, both in the structure of the pieces and in the concepts that they convey. Because of the many hours that it takes for quilts to evolve, I have time to reflect on my use of fragmented imagery. I believe this relates to a personal philosophy, based on my own experiences, that life is a very textured, colorful event complete with unwanted tragedy and exhilarating happiness. I can list many events that have influenced my personality, and I believe that these memories are fragments of a past that also influences my work.

As I develop the language of my work, I experiment continually with my imagery. Often this involves moving from abstracted representation to recognizable imagery and back. By challenging the expressiveness of fragments and simple lines, I expand my vocabulary. ⇨

Further reading

These books contain helpful information and exercises for quilt designers.

Gutcheon, Jeffrey. **Diamond Patchwork.** New York: Alchemy Press, 1982.

Horton, Roberta. **An Amish Adventure: A Workbook for Color in Quilts.** Lafayette, CA: C & T Publishers, 1983.

Horton, Roberta. **Calico and Beyond: The Use of Patterned Fabrics in Quilts.** Lafayette, CA: C & T Publishers, 1986.

James, Michael. **The Second Quiltmaker's Handbook: Creative Approaches to Contemporary Quilt Design.** Englewood Cliffs, NJ: Prentice-Hall, 1981.

The following books provide an excellent overview of contemporary quilt art.

Crow, Nancy. **Nancy Crow, Quilts and Influences.** Paducah, KY: American Quilter's Society, 1990.

McMorris, Penny and Michael Kile. **The Art Quilt.** San Francisco, CA: Quilt Digest Press, 1986.

The New Quilt #1: The Dairy Barn Quilt National. Newtown, CT: The Taunton Press, 1991.

Porcella, Yvonne. **A Colorful Book.** Modesto, CA: Porcella Studios, 1986.

Sources of inspiration

Most often I get my ideas directly from nature. So many times a simple glance outside has led to another quilt. From my window I look out to my yard with its magnolias, plums, junipers, firs, rhododendrons, and azaleas. Across the street are more trees: apple, blue spruce, laurel, maple, and cherry. Layered in the distance are the blues of Lake Washington, the greens of Mercer Island, more Lake Washington blues, the city of Seattle, and, on a clear day, the Olympic Mountains showing in the background. I study these infinitely variable colors, textures, lines, and shapes, paying particular attention to how they change with the changes in weather, the time of day, and the seasons.

My family's tradition of artistic expression has been an inspiration to me from my earliest years, in particular my mother's ongoing painting career. The photography in nature books and magazines allows me to go places I can't personally experience. Visiting galleries and museums and studying fine arts and crafts allows me to learn from other artists' interpretations of their experiences.

Occasionally, music has served as inspiration for my more abstract works. "Hot Licks" was created in honor of my late uncle Chuck Wells, a jazz trumpet player who possessed an enormous range. "Musing Mahler" was inspired by watching "Live at Lincoln Center"—bits of contrasting bright colors against a gray background suggest musical notes bursting from instruments.

I believe that if you *want* inspiration, you *will* find it. You need an open, receptive mind and the persistence to pursue it. Just as in developing an individual language, it takes hard work, time, and a combination of intellectual evaluation and working from the heart. □

Erika Carter is a quilt artist whose award-winning work has been exhibited around the world. (Quilt photos by Howard Carter)

As Carter pursued her tree images, they became progressively more recognizable, without becoming more realistic. "Reaching" (47 in. by 67 in.; 1989), at right, is also an effort to express more of the human element, as the spreading branches mimic the impulse to aspire, and to grow. "Birches" (35½ in. by 55 in.; 1990), above, reverses many of the elements of Carter's earlier work. Here the trees are represented only by their hand-appliquéd trunks; branches and leaves, up to now the sole ingredients in her tree quilts, are completely absent, but implied. She also uses the inspiration of birch trees to experiment with light shapes against a dark background.

Quilting the Big Picture

Bleached, painted, and stippled fabrics add realism to appliquéd images

by Velda Newman

From *Threads* magazine (July 1992) 41:38-41

you could say I'm a painter who loves fabric more than paint, since I trained as a visual artist, and what I'm most interested in is designing with color and natural imagery. Discovering that I could design in fabric brought all my enthusiasms together, and when I realized that I could also manipulate the color and texture of fabrics with inks, dyes, and bleach, as well as with quilting, I became a total convert.

Each of my large-scale, plant-inspired appliqué quilts, like "California," shown on the facing page, takes about a year to complete: three months to design, six or seven months to appliqué, and three months to quilt and finish. You don't need a year to get fascinating results from bleach and paint on fabric, though. All you need is a free afternoon and a spirit of adventure—but here's what I do:

Color and design

When I plan a quilt, I start with color. I'm always on the lookout for wonderful colors in combination, like the golden California poppies and violet-blue lupines I see near my home in the spring. In "California," for example, I knew that I wanted to use rich purples, greens, and yellows. Then I selected images that called for those colors.

Next, I make sketches. When I've got one I like, I trace it onto 1/4-in. graph paper using a light box, and then enlarge it to full size on 1-in. pattern paper. An idea may look great small, but when I blow it up to 7 by 8 ft., I get a whole new perspective. I often wind up making major changes in the full-size drawing.

I want to catch the viewer's eye with color, then lure them in for a closer look. But the big picture comes first, and for me that means great color and strong shapes. When you see a quilt across the room with a knockout color combination and powerful design, you'll want to go over and look at that one, and only then will you see the fine points, the appliqué, the quilting, and the quality of the workmanship. I try to make my quilts interesting from any distance.

Most of my quilts are floral because flowers are my greatest inspiration. I get ideas from everywhere: live plants from my garden or a nursery, books, even from greeting cards. I often refer to photos to see the details in a leaf or flower.

Bleached areas of fabrics add visual depth to the fruits and leaves in Velda Newman's quilt "California," shown on the facing page. Bleach is easy to use, as Newman describes.

Fabrics

I use only all-cotton fabrics because blends are harder to appliqué with; their edges tend to pop out when folded under, while cottons crease easily and stay put nicely. My stash of fabrics isn't huge, but I'm forever watching out for unusual colors to add to my collection. I buy mostly solids, sometimes in a range of colors.

All of my quilts contain fabrics I've dyed and bleached, and occasionally you'll find some painting in them as well. This way I can get effects that aren't possible with appliqué alone. By manipulating the fabric's color and texture myself, I can get a more realistic look—an individual petal on a flower, lifelike veining on a leaf. You can see the kind of effects I'm after in the lower left photos on p. 88.

Bleach effects—You'll be amazed at what happens when you bleach fabrics. The colors you wind up with depend entirely on the base color of the fabric. I've seen one brown fabric bleached to a muted pink, while a similar soft gold bleached to a yellow green. It's not an exact science. You have to play around to get the effects you want, and you've got to be careful not to damage the fabric by overbleaching; if the color doesn't come up just the way I want within 60 seconds, I toss the fabric out. (Be sure to protect your clothes, eyes, and work surface when using bleach.) As soon as the color is right, immediately dunk the fabric in warm, sudsy water and rinse it out thoroughly.

As you can see in the top photo on p. 88, the tools needed for bleaching are simple—brushes and squirt and spray bottles. You can use full-strength or diluted bleach; it depends on the look you want. If I need a strong light/dark contrast in a shape, like the reddish-brown pear in "California," I'll apply the bleach full strength. In that quilt I also bleached a commercial purple-and-black print to get reddish-purple highlights, with the black still in, for some of the grapes: they're shown in the center detail photo on p. 88.

On the grapes in "California," I wanted definite highlights, so I put on droplets of bleach with a small squirt bottle with a snip-off point. At the center of each spot, where the bleach was most concentrated, the color is lightest; as the bleach bled outward, the color stayed darker. If you work on wet fabric, the bleach spreads farther, like watercolors on wet paper. Occasionally, I'll put down a bead of bleach and then use a brush to blend it out.

If you want a contoured look, use a spray bottle that mists. The brown/pink pear in "California" shows what happens when you saturate the fabric with bleach:

Color comes out uniformly. By using less bleach and spraying in a sweeping motion, you get a speckled, contoured look.

Painting—I use watered down artists' acrylics to create darker contours. If I thin the paint enough, it won't stiffen the fabric and I get the staining effect I'm after. Sometimes, after I've bleached the fabric, I'll go back and paint in another color with acrylics. I also occasionally use felt-tip pens to create subtle shading. (I use Deka Fabric Markers and Pigma Pens by Nicron.) I'll work with the pen on its side to blur a line and make a soft shadow, or perhaps I'll make random dots to add detail that you only see close up. I do the ink work as I'm doing the quilting.

Working on the wall

Once I've got the fabrics I want, I attach them to my full-size drawing. First I pin the drawing to a large piece of fiberboard that covers most of one of my studio walls. Then I cut out the shapes and pin them right to the drawing, working from the background layers of the composition to the foreground. The smaller, simpler shapes, such as individual grapes, I'll cut freehand. But for larger or more intricate pieces, I trace the shape from the drawing onto another piece of paper, which I cut out and use like a pattern.

Sometimes what looked good as a drawing just doesn't work with the actual fabrics, so as the pieces get pinned to the wall, I step back often to evaluate the design, and I keep moving the pieces, changing their positions from the drawing. It took me almost a month to find the right spot for the pears in "California."

I also use a reducing glass (available from Katie's Collection, Rancho Alegre, Santa Fe, NM 87505; 505-471-2899) to give me a better sense of how the colors and shapes work together. My quilts need to be seen from at least 10 feet away to get the whole picture, and I can't get that far back from the wall in my studio. With the reducing glass, I can stand closer to the quilt and still see it as I hope others will.

Up to this point, I've been working against the white of the drawing paper, but when I'm satisfied with the appliqué design, I take down the pieces and pin up the background fabric I think I'll want. I lightly chalk mark a 1-ft. grid on the fabric to help me in pinning the pieces again. I put the full-size drawing on an adjacent wall and look back and forth from fabric to drawing as I repin, but by now I'm pretty sure where all the pieces go because I've moved them so many times.

The background fabric is critical; it can kill the design or bring it to life. Often I'll

To control the effect of bleach on commercial and hand-dyed fabric, Newman sprays, brushes, and squirts the bleach in the shapes she wants. She keeps a bowl of water nearby to rinse off the bleach before it does too much damage to the fabric.

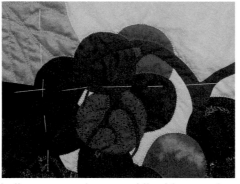

In the grapes above and the blossoms below, you can see the results of bleaching. Newman uses contour and stipple quilting in the leaf and pear at left for additional texture and to enhance the realism.

try two or three different colors before finding the one that works. I must have tried six different colors on "Hydrangea," on the facing page, before I settled on the yellow; all the other colors I tried dulled the colors of the blossoms, but that bright yellow really brought them out. With the right background in place, I might move a few more pieces around, but then I take the pins out of the fiberboard and pin each piece to just the background fabric.

Doing the appliqué

Once I design a quilt, the rest is rote, especially the appliqué. There are some design possibilities still to come with the quilting, which I love to explore, but the appliqué process is strictly mechanical. Unfortunately, it also takes the most time. I work in the same order that I pinned, from the bottom layer up. As I stitch, I catch only the immediate fabric underneath, so I can later cut away the layers from the back to reduce bulk.

I turn the raw edge of the appliqué under with the needle as I go. I use a No. 10 Clover quilting needle for both appliqué and quilting, and I appliqué with Metrosene cotton thread. I also use a round magnifying lamp on a stand, which helps a great deal when I'm appliquéing dark colors. I try to keep my stitching very close—especially on curves—because if I don't, the pieces shift when I start to quilt.

For each large piece, I've traced a paper pattern from my large drawing, then cut around it on the fabric, adding a ⅜-in. seam allowance as I cut. I turn under only ⅛ in. when I appliqué, but I like to have a little extra in case I decide to slightly change the shape as I'm working. With such freeform shapes, nothing needs to be that exact. I can trim off any extra fabric, and if I find that some pieces are a little short, I just add another element. I can play with the parts like this up until the pre-appliqué basting.

I baste the pieces somewhat haphazardly, making sure not to catch the edges that will be turned under when I appliqué. Then, using my needle, I turn under about ⅛ in. and place my stitches very close so that they really hold.

When at long last the appliqué is finished, I begin cutting away the layers from the back. I hang the quilt top, with the wrong side facing inside, in front of a sliding glass door so the light shows through and I can see the different layers. With small, very sharp sewing scissors, I begin cutting away the bottom layer, continuing until I get to the layer on top on the right side. I cut to within ⅛ in. of the appliqué stitching, which is another reason I keep my appliqué stitches very close. I only cut during the day, when I have good light, and the process can easily take two weeks.

Backing and basting

At this point I decide on my backing fabric. Some of my quilts have a plain backing, but lately I've experimented with backings that are a part of the quilt design. For "Hydrangea," I used plaids that picked up colors in the appliqué; for "California," I chose a commercial print of grape clusters and leaves.

Next I layer the backing, a low-loft poly batting, and quilt top, and baste them together. I keep my basting fairly loose but close (about 4 in. both ways) because I quilt in a hoop and it gets moved a lot.

Quilting

I quilt with cotton-wrapped polyester thread because I find it shreds and knots less than cotton, and I use a 24-in. oval hoop rather than a frame because a frame takes up so much space and you have to work on it wherever the frame is set up. With my hoop and magnifying lamp, I can curl up wherever there's a chair and quilt for hours at a time.

When I begin quilting, I don't have a set design in mind. I put the quilt in the hoop and mark quilting lines with a purple disappearing pen. (I've used that pen on all my quilts and have never had a problem.) I mark and quilt as I go. Outline quilting sets off a shape, contour quilting within a shape defines it, and stipple quilting creates shadows and texture. To help form a large area like the yellow pear in "California," I did contour quilting inside the shape. To accentuate the mottled appearance of the large brown leaf, I added stipple quilting to the lighter areas.

I'll use quilting thread that matches the color of the fabric if I want to add texture or dimension without breaking up the color, or I'll use a different thread, especially a darker one, to make shadows or bring up small dots of color. With all my quilting, I hope to create small surprises that are seen later, on a closer look.

Edgings and bindings

I don't even think about the edging or binding until the quilting is done and I can take a good long look at the nearly finished piece. I may choose to bind it in a color that's in the quilt. In that case, I want to finish the edge without adding another design element. It's more likely that I'll edge the quilt with a few narrow strips of contrasting color before the binding is sewn on. Contrast edging can really spark the colors and make a frame that sets off the quilt. On "Hydrangea," you'd expect a green binding, but instead I chose colors that are unpredictable, even outrageous: red and fuchsia for edging, black and white for binding. Some people look at them with surprise, but I think those two strips of brilliant color are just what the quilt needed. The hydrangeas are so flowery, with all that blue, yellow, and green, that I wanted something almost jarring on the edge. The strong, precise lines make a graphic contrast to a quilt that's full of rounded forms.

Edgings and bindings are easy, and I do them in a similar way, as shown in the drawing below. I prefer double-layer binding because it's more substantial and easier to apply than a binding with a pressed-under raw edge. I'm always on the watch for black-and-white striped fabric to use for binding. I like the idea of dyeing the striped fabric a color that's in the quilt so the white becomes part of the quilt and the black remains in contrast. □

Veida Newman's quilt "California" was recently awarded Best in Show at the American International Quilt Association show in Houston, Texas.

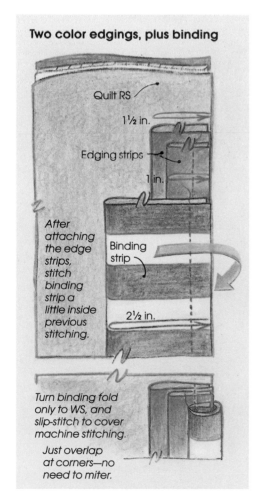

Two color edgings, plus binding

Quilt RS

1½ in.

Edging strips

1 in.

After attaching the edge strips, stitch binding strip a little inside previous stitching.

Binding strip

2½ in.

Turn binding fold only to WS, and slip-stitch to cover machine stitching.

Just overlap at corners—no need to miter.

Newman experimented with six different background colors before deciding on the brilliant yellow of "Hydrangea" (84 by 99 in.; 1989), winner of first prize at the annual competition of the American Quilter's Society, in Paducah, KY.

Caring for Quilts

An intimate visit with two of America's most passionate collectors

by Virginia Avery

From *Threads* magazine (September 1991) 36:76-79

a very private home at the end of a long, secluded lane seems an unlikely place to find several hundred antique and contemporary quilts housed in a specially built, climate-controlled gallery. Yet these are the surroundings of the Ardis and Robert James Collection, a treasury of fine needlework.

In the more than 10 years they have been acquiring quilts, the Jameses have set a precedent by building a unique and fascinating collection of both antique and contemporary quilts. They feel that the present is intertwined with the past, and that the needle and thread are as valid in reporting and recording history as the pen.

About 10 years ago, Ardis went to a quilt festival in Troy, Michigan, and saw a Mariner's Compass quilt. It was love at first sight, and she bought it.

Ardis returned to the quilt festival in Troy the following year, and bought two quilts; the year after, she bought four, and Bob's encouragement and enthusiasm led him to join her in the next shopping expedition. They returned with 32 quilts. They were no longer now-and-then purchasers; they had become dyed-in-the-wool collectors.

It wasn't long, of course, before the house was filled. Quilts were hung on every available wall, the stairwell, and the stair railing. They were folded on the couch, displayed on specially built racks, and spilling out of closets. They were stacked 25 and 30 deep on the guest beds, and suddenly the Jameses were faced with the decision to either stop collecting or find more space. "In a way, it really wasn't a decision; we never considered stopping the collection," Ardis said.

They decided to add on above their three-car garage. It was two years and four sets of architectural plans before the addition, built to museum specifications, became a reality.

The gallery, 22 ft. by 33 ft., is completely sealed. No plants, pets, or foods are permitted inside. An air conditioner and an air cleaner, both state of the art, control the climate. The light is also controlled, dark enough to protect the quilts and light enough to satisfy the viewer. Anyone handling the quilts must wear white gloves.

Although quilts hang on all the walls, the majority of them are stacked flat on four enormous hardwood platforms. Smaller quilts are stacked flat on wheeled carts that slide under the platforms, trundle-bed fashion. Many antique quilts show damage along crease lines caused by being stored folded in quarters. Flat storage prevents any further harm of this kind. If the quilts must be folded for any reason, Ardis folds them in thirds, lengthwise and crosswise, to avoid putting any stress on the original crease lines.

Serious responsibility goes hand in hand with any substantial collection. Ardis and Bob have a highly organized and sophisticated system of record keeping. Each quilt is numbered as it comes into the house, then photographed. The provenance, condition, and any other pertinent details are carefully entered into a loose-leaf logbook. This hand-recorded appraisal is also entered into a computer system.

The advice of Michael Kile, founder and publisher of Quilt Digest Press (955 14th St., San Francisco, CA 94114), has had a significant influence on the Jameses' classic quilt acquisitions. For contemporary quilts, Bob and Ardis have consulted art historian and author Penny McMorris. Quilt dealers Joe Sarah and Sandra Mitchell have each represented the Jameses' interests in quilt purchases.

They do not buy quilts that are in need of extensive repairs, but a trained conservator does make small repairs. She does not replace any missing fabric or worn bindings, but will stabilize such damaged areas by covering them with netting so the quilt can be displayed.

Because the Jameses buy only what appeals to them, their collection has a unique personality. Ardis listens to her heart; quilts have a strong emotional appeal for her and she is able to make up her mind almost instantly. Bob is only slightly

Inside the James Gallery (at left), traditional and contemporary quilts hang side by side. To preserve their unique collection, the Jameses have devised a clever method of flat storage: On four large platforms and the trundles under them, several hundred quilts rest, awaiting their turn to be admired. The quilted screen in the background is "The Precipice," by Gayle Fraas and Duncan Slade. (Photos by Susan Kahn)

Broderie perse means "Persian embroidery," but not all broderie perse quilts were embroidered. The term describes the technique of cutting designs from printed chintz and appliquéing them on a background. This broderie perse was signed by Eliza Thompson of Virginia or South Carolina in 1809. After applying the designs to muslin, Eliza used trapunto to emphasize the grapes and leaves of the quilting, and to echo the appliquéd brown vines. (100 in. by 102 in.)

The expressive figures in this detail from "My Crazy Dream" (above) are embroidered in satin stitch, tied satin stitch, and backstitch on a shaded satin patch about 5 in. square. The Erl King and the abducted child are characters from a poem popular in Victorian times. M.M. Hernandred Ricard made her amazing crazy quilt (left) from satins, velvets, brocades, and ribbons, between 1877 and 1912. She included her picture (probably transferred to fabric by lithography) in the lower right, along with details like the spider trapping a fly in the upper left. The decorative stitching around each crazy piece shows off her wonderful repertoire of embroidery techniques. (65 in. by 60 in.)

more cautious; he respects Ardis' intuition, but he looks for fine workmanship and attention to detail as well.

The scope of the collection is enormous. The oldest quilt they have dates from the late 1700s. They own three Baltimore album quilts, one a very rare *broderie perse*-Baltimore album combination. Another James *broderie perse*, a more usual example of the technique, is shown on the preceeding page. They have one of five classic quilts a Mrs. Carpenter made for her grandchildren. All five are based on the Milky Way and the path of the moon through the sky. The one the Jameses own was packed away by the Carpenter family when the child for whom it was made died, and it is in mint condition.

One recent acquisition is a fun- and surprise-filled calendar quilt made by Susan Shie. The days, months, and holidays all button on a grid on the quilt, so they can be changed at will.

Some time ago they were approached by a representative of the Kokusai Art Co. and Mitsukoshi department stores of Japan about lending quilts for an exhibit to travel

Exquisite quilting distinguishes this "Princess Feather," made in about 1870 by an unknown artisan. The red and green feather borders, medallions, and eagles are appliquéd to the white ground, but accented by reverse appliqué in the central ribs of the feathers and wing details of the eagles. The pattern name evolved from "Prince's feather," a reference to the heraldic emblem of the Prince of Wales. (96 in. by 96 in.)

to seven cities in Japan for almost a year. The 40 antique and 10 contemporary quilts have returned from their goodwill tour. "I missed them," Ardis says. "I miss all the quilts when they're away; they're like children. I'm glad to have them home again, but I'm glad so many people have had a chance to see them, too. It's a cultural exchange between countries, and anything like this helps us all understand each other a little better."

At present, there are no exhibits planned for the U.S. or abroad, but negotiations are open. Individuals can arrange to visit the collection by appointment, but the gallery is small and doesn't accommodate groups. For more information, write to Mr. and Mrs. James in care of *Threads*, 63 S. Main St., PO Box 5506, Newtown, CT 06470-5506. □

Virginia Avery is a designer of quilts and art clothing. She is the author of The Big Book of Appliqué *(out of print),* Quilts to Wear *(recently reprinted by Dover Publications), and* Wonderful Wearables: A Celebration of Creative Clothing *(to be released in September).*

Thousands of tiny wool diamonds and squares were meticulously pieced together by the maker of this surprisingly modern looking "Star Mosaic." The angles of the diamonds within the blocks form a subtle three-dimensional illusion. Four rows of full diamonds were stitched into the borders, overlapping the maroon backing, which shows as a row of half-diamonds at the edges. (62 in. by 77 in.)

Index

If you enjoyed this book, you'll love our magazine.

A year's subscription to *Threads* brings you the kind of hands-on information you found in this book, and much more. In issue after issue—six times a year—you'll discover articles on sewing, quilting, knitting and other needlecrafts. Artists and professionals share their best techniques and trade secrets with you. With detailed illustrations and full-color photographs that bring each project to life, *Threads* will inspire you to create your best work ever!

To subscribe, just fill out one of the attached subscription cards or call us toll free at 1-800-888-8286.

The Taunton Press Guarantee

If you are not completely satisfied you may cancel at any time and we'll immediately refund your payment in full.

Taunton
BOOKS & VIDEOS
for fellow enthusiasts

The Taunton Press 63 S. Main Street, P.O. Box 5506, Newtown, CT 06470-5506

Threads

Use this card to subscribe to *Threads* or to request information about other Taunton Press magazines, books and videos.

☐ 1 year (6 issues) for just $28—over 15% off the newsstand price. Outside the U.S. $34/year (U.S. funds, please. Canadian residents: GST included)

☐ 2 years (12 issues) for just $48—27% off the newsstand price. Outside the U.S. $56/year (U.S. funds, please. Canadian residents: GST included)

Name ______________________

Address ______________________

City ______________________

State ______________ Zip ________

☐ My payment is enclosed. ☐ Please bill me.

☐ Please send me information about other Taunton Press magazines, books and videos. (BBBS)

I'm interested in:

1 ☐ sewing
2 ☐ embroidery
3 ☐ woodworking
4 ☐ gardening
5 ☐ knitting
6 ☐ quilting
7 ☐ home building
8 ☐ other

BTH6

Threads

Use this card to subscribe to *Threads* or to request information about other Taunton Press magazines, books and videos.

☐ 1 year (6 issues) for just $28—over 15% off the newsstand price. Outside the U.S. $34/year (U.S. funds, please. Canadian residents: GST included)

☐ 2 years (12 issues) for just $48—27% off the newsstand price. Outside the U.S. $56/year (U.S. funds, please. Canadian residents: GST included)

Name ______________________

Address ______________________

City ______________________

State ______________ Zip ________

☐ My payment is enclosed. ☐ Please bill me.

☐ Please send me information about other Taunton Press magazines, books and videos. (BBBS)

I'm interested in:

1 ☐ sewing
2 ☐ embroidery
3 ☐ woodworking
4 ☐ gardening
5 ☐ knitting
6 ☐ quilting
7 ☐ home building
8 ☐ other

BTH6

Taunton
BOOKS & VIDEOS
for fellow enthusiasts

NO POSTAGE
NECESSARY
IF MAILED
IN THE
UNITED STATES

BUSINESS REPLY MAIL
FIRST CLASS MAIL PERMIT NO.19 NEWTOWN, CT

POSTAGE WILL BE PAID BY ADDRESSEE

Threads®
63 SOUTH MAIN STREET
PO BOX 5506
NEWTOWN CT 06470-9976

Taunton
BOOKS & VIDEOS
for fellow enthusiasts

NO POSTAGE
NECESSARY
IF MAILED
IN THE
UNITED STATES

BUSINESS REPLY MAIL
FIRST CLASS MAIL PERMIT NO.19 NEWTOWN, CT

POSTAGE WILL BE PAID BY ADDRESSEE

Threads®
63 SOUTH MAIN STREET
PO BOX 5506
NEWTOWN CT 06470-9976